Dancing and Mixed Media

NEW STUDIES IN AESTHETICS

Robert Ginsberg
General Editor

Vol. 17

PETER LANG
New York • San Francisco • Bern • Baltimore
Frankfurt am Main • Berlin • Wien • Paris

Judith B. Alter

Dancing and Mixed Media

Early Twentieth-Century Modern Dance Theory in Text and Photography

PETER LANG

New York • San Francisco • Bern • Baltimore
Frankfurt am Main • Berlin • Wien • Paris

Library of Congress Cataloging-in-Publication Data

Alter, Judith B.
  Dancing and mixed media : early twentieth-century modern dance theory
in text and photography / Judith B. Alter.
      p.   cm. — (New studies in aesthetics ; vol. 17)
  Includes bibliographical references (p.) and index.
  1. Modern dance—Philosophy—History—20th century. 2. Dancing—
Social aspects—History—20th century. I. Title. II. Series.
  GV1783.A48   1994   792.8—dc20   93-2968
  ISBN 0-8204-2167-7   CIP
  ISSN 0893-6005

Die Deutsche Bibliothek-CIP-Einheitsaufnahme

Alter, Judith B.:
Dancing and mixed media : early twentieth-century modern dance theory in
text and photography / Judith B. Alter. - New York; Bern; Frankfurt/M.;
Paris; Wien: Lang, 1994
   (New studies in aesthetics ; Vol. 17)
   ISBN 0-8204-2167-7
NE: GT

The paper in this book meets the guidelines for permanence and durability of
the Committee on Production Guidelines for Book Longevity of the
Council on Library Resources.

© Peter Lang Publishing, Inc., New York 1994

Printed in the United States of America.

Table of Contents

List of Illustrations

(Plates begin on page 111)

Preface

I trace the origin of this book back to 1985 when I first analyzed and wrote a paper about the books by Charles and Caroline Caffin and J.E. Crawford Flitch. I titled the paper, "An Analysis of Two Coffee-Table Dance Books From 1912," because I believed that the number of photographs in each of their books—forty-seven—was unusual for that time. Now I know that my intuition about the number and special quality of the photographs was sound. To substantiate the accuracy of my observation, I learned much more about books: their construction and layout, their publishers and readers, and their photographers and photographs.

I put aside the paper about the books by the Caffins and Flitch and continued my study of dance theory written from 1930 to 1970, published in *Dance-Based Dance Theory* (1991). When examining books about early modern dance written between 1903 and 1926, I discovered quite a few which had a large number of photographs. One by one, I analyzed the theoretical concepts in these books, uncovering many common threads they shared with the books I had examined in *Dance-Based Dance Theory*. First I analyzed the educational dance theory of Mary Beegle (published in *Dance: Current Selected Research*, Volume IV) whose ideas and teaching markedly influenced her more well-known colleagues and students: Gertrude Colby, founder of the dance program at Columbia Teachers College in 1928; Bird Larson, who taught "Natural Rhythmic Expression" at the Neighborhood Playhouse in New York City from the late 1910s to the late 1920s; and Margaret H'Doubler, who established the first dance major at the University of Wisconsin in 1927.

In my classes at the University of California-Los Angeles I had been teaching the theoretical ideas of Isadora Duncan. I had analyzed her writings using the "Framework of Topics Intrinsic to Dance Theory," the method of analysis I had worked out in my study of nineteen writers, aestheticians, and dancers, who wrote about dance between 1930 and 1971 (published in *Dance-Based Dance Theory*). The Framework emerged from and then helped to organize the dance topics these writers discussed. In that book, the Framework was a tool for organizing ideas and a tool of analysis. It has also served as an analytical tool for the examination of the material in this book.

Separately I analyzed the books by Helen Moller, Margaret Morris, Eleanor Elder, Margaret H'Doubler (written in 1921 and 1925), and an essay by Raymond Duncan (see Appendix for Glenna Josephson's translation of that essay). I put those analyses alongside my studies of the ideas of Isadora Duncan and Mary Beegle. Using the topics of the Framework, I made a chart to see more clearly the similarities and differences in the ideas of these several thinkers. I found similarities but I also found that none of them talked about some issues which became central in dance theoretical writing in the 1930s, 1940s, and 1950s: the dance itself in performance, the kinesthetic sense, and the study of most features of the dance experience. I finally understood why the word "dancing" recurred in most of the titles of their books: the interests of the authors centered more on the activity of dancing than on the dance itself or on the academic field of dance, with its focus on documentation, preservation, and analysis. In the process of analyzing the ideas of each dancer-writer I was compelled to investigate the recurrent themes which emerged from their writing: the return to nature, an idealization of Greek life and art, rhythm as the great organizing force in nature, the sentiments against ballet and popular dance, art-making as the way to achieve the good life, and the arts as basic education. Gaining an understanding of these themes clarified why the dancer-writers said what they said in the way they said it. Many of their ideas sound strange to us today, but, in the cultural context of that time, the arguments make sense and help explain developments in modern dance theory which followed.

What about the photographs? Photography as an artistic medium was emerging at the same time as early modern dance. As this study shows, by utilizing dance photographs in their books the dancer-writers (as I refer to the authors listed above) helped spread the word and sell ideas about both dance and photography. The books themselves as media disseminated the visual message which helped convey the kinesthetic impact of dancing. As a major subject of this book I examine the success of these messages and media.

In this book I investigate the same period in dance history as Nancy Ruyter's *Reformers and Visionaries* (1979), Elizabeth Kendall's *Where She Danced* (1979) and Naima Prevots's *American Pageantry: A Movement for Art and Democracy* (1990). I am indebted to them, their insight, and their books. This volume overlaps with their books but does not duplicate them. By analyzing the texts of seven dancer-writers my book further develops the insights of Kendall, Ruyter, and Prevots, adds new ideas, introduces a broader context, and examines the relationship of the books, photographs, technique systems, and schools to the dancing these early modern dancers were developing.

Readers from many disciplines will enjoy reading *Dancing and Mixed Media*: students, scholars, and laypeople interested in dance, American studies, American and European intellectual history, photography, art, and social history. This book interrelates the analysis of texts with the cultural context in which the authors lived and worked. By starting with the dancer-writers' words, ideas, and media, this inductive study highlights the major cultural factors which influenced the shaping of early twentieth-century modern dance and modern dance theory.

The dancer-writers call the new kind of dancing they advocated by a variety of names: "classical," derived from classical Greece; "natural," based on movements everyone can do, such as walking, running, hopping, and skipping; "interpretive," based on the dancer's emotional and physical interpretation of music; "free," not bound by any traditional technique system, and "barefoot" referring to the daring—in late Victorian terms—exposure of the dancers' feet.

This sampling of books and essays about "dancing" includes: Raymond Duncan's essay "Dancing and Gymnastics" (1914), the two-part chapter on dance in Mary Porter Beegle and Jack Randall Crawford's *Community Drama and Pageantry* (1916), Helen Moller's *Dancing with Helen Moller* (1918), Eleanor Elder's *Dance, A National Art* (1918), Margaret H'Doubler's *A Manual of Dancing* (1921) and *The Dance and Its Place in Education* (1925), Margaret Morris's *Margaret Morris Dancing* (1926), and Isadora Duncan's book of collected writings, *The Art of the Dance* (1929).

To supplement the picture of dancing written by practitioners, I examine a few books by critic-photographers who write about or photograph the dancing they saw during the first thirty years of the twentieth century: J. E. Crawford Flitch's *Modern Dancing and Dancers* (1912), Charles and Caroline Caffin's *Dancing and Dancers of Today* (1912), and Arnold Genthe's *The Book of the Dance* (1916). In both groups of books photographs play a significant part in conveying the authors' message about dancing. During this same period when natural dancing was developing into an art in its own right, artist-photographers struggled to have photography recognized as an autonomous art form. The mutual support of dance and photography produces a intriguing picture of these two developing arts.

This study is divided into three sections. Chapters 1 and 2 contains two kinds of background: the first examines the predominant cultural forces which influence the dancer-writers and provides a context for their ideas, while the second presents the biographical background of the dancer-writers and a brief style description of their books, essays, or pamphlets. The analysis of the texts, Chapters 3–8, contains the topics which the dancers examine in their books: dancing in its social and historical contexts; the body, movement, and dance movement; composition, performance, and the other arts; and support systems which contributed to the development of this new art—technique or movement systems, and dance education. In these chapters, the ideas of each writer are collected, examined, and compared. In Chapters 9 and 10, I examine the media: the photography and the books themselves were the primary media which the dancer-writers utilized to promote their vision of their new form of dancing.

Since all these books are now in the public domain I am able to reproduce the photographs included here. I am glad that I can circulate them again to interested readers at the end of the century in which they first appeared. My thanks go to the people in photographic services at Dance Collection, the New York Public Library for the Performing Arts, Astor, Lenox, and Tilden Foundations for photographing and granting permission to reprint the pictures in Eleanor Elder's book. I am deeply grateful to my editor Randy Woodland, Lecturer in the Writing Programs at the University of California-Los Angeles, who gently urged me to reconfigure my initial series of essays into the cohesive unit this book has become and who expertly guided my revisions and designed the camera-ready manuscript. I appreciate his patience, wisdom, and continued interest in these topics. I am also grateful to Georgette Schneer for her friendship and help in locating material for me from the Dance Collection at Lincoln Center. Deep appreciation also goes to my friend and former colleague Ann Devaney, Professor of Educational Technology at the University of Wisconsin in Madison, whose keen eye and love of dance combined to suggest the way I analyzed the many photographs in these books. I want to thank Glenna Josephson, M. A., for her careful and sensitive translation of the essay by Raymond Duncan used here. Also I appreciate the many hours the reference librarians in the University of California-Los Angeles, University of California-Riverside, and University of Wisconsin-Madison Libraries spent with me looking, often to no avail, for biographical information and birth and death dates for some of these dancer-writers. The Research Committee of the Academic Senate at the University of California-Los Angeles gave me a grant to cover the costs of making the negatives for the plates in this book; to the members of the committee I extend my deep appreciation. And I am delighted to work again with Robert Ginsberg, editor of the Peter Lang Series, New Studies in Aesthetics. His patience, knowledge, suggestions, expertise, and support have been indispensable for this project, and I am deeply grateful to him.

1

Cultural Forces Influencing Dancing

The Social and Political Context

The development of early modern dance as a new form of theater dance reflects the social, political, educational, and artistic transitions occurring in American and European society at the end of the nineteenth and the first part of the twentieth century. These changes took place on several levels of society and in many spheres of activity. An overview of the time, often labelled "late Victorian," provides the backdrop for understanding the phenomenon of early modern dance. Much of the introductory information gathered here comes from interdisciplinary fields of intellectual history and the newly recognized area of social history, the history of how people—men, women, and children—live, work, play, dress, and interact. Historians in these disciplines have analyzed Victorian values, and their insights introduce this study of "dancing" in the early twentieth century. (See Cobern, Schlereth, Smith, and Walvin).

Victorian Values

The term "Victorian times" refers to the historical period of sixty years during which Queen Victoria reigned in Great Britain, 1837-1901, when British leaders formalized their Empire and British and other European rulers established their colonies in many areas of the world. The term "Victorian" more broadly refers to a wide variety of attitudes toward life which converged during this period in Western history, though many of the stated-values oversimplified complex and ongoing issues in the lives of the people at that time. A set of social and moral values or an ideal description of character frequently come to mind with the mention of the adjective "Victorian." In *Victorian Values* (1987) James Walvin identifies these: close family life, thrift, piety, chastity, hard work, obedience to superiors, cleanliness, and love of country. Most of these values predated this time in history. Though the multitude of different reformers who offered solutions to the serious problems of this time preached these values, their importance came more from necessity than the striving of people to follow an ideal code of behavior. In reality, people needed to *work hard* to earn enough money to live, they needed *thrift* to survive on low wages, *chastity* could prevent disease and limit the number of young mouths one had to feed, and so on.

Stanley Coben in *Rebellion Against Victorianism* (1991) identifies the virtues associated with true Victorian character. Both males and females must be

> dependably self-controlled, punctual, orderly, hardworking, conscien-
> tious, sober, respectful of other Victorians' property rights, ready to
> postpone immediate gratification for long-term goals, pious toward a
> usually friendly God, a believer in the truth of the Bible, oriented strongly
> toward home and family, honorable in relations with other Victorians,
> anxious for self-improvement in a fashion which might appear compul-
> sive to modern observers and patriotic. (Coben, 1991:4)

Reformers of the working class, teachers, parents, politicians, and spiritual
leaders from many denominations preached about benefits of these character
traits and sought ways to instill them in their target populations. The social
values Walvin identifies and the personality characteristics Cobern cites overlap. Both social historians agree that the stress on these ideals arose not because
they prevailed but because they did *not* predominate in peoples' lives or
behavior. The "reformer" manner in which the early twentieth-century dancer-
writers, analyzed here, extol the value of dancing reflects the practice of other
reformers who offered solutions to life's problems.

During this historical period serious problems confronted the lives of the
majority of European and American citizens. Cities had haphazardly grown in
size and population at a rate unknown in previous times, often doubling or
tripling primarily because of the growth of industry. Industries offered jobs to
people who came from farm and rural settings to take them. Workers lived
anywhere they could find to live: often in crowded, unsafe, unhygienic, ugly
living quarters. To pay the rent in these living quarters, children and women as
well as men worked long hours for low wages in factories which had inadequate
light, heat, and ventilation.

To improve the lives of the working classes, leaders and visionaries
propounded political solutions for their many problems. During the last third
of the nineteenth century and the beginning of the twentieth, observers applied
the term "progressive" to those politicians and to leaders in fields such as
education and clothing reform who worked to improve the social conditions of
the working people. Over time they brought about changes: workers organized
labor unions, city managers built sanitation facilities, and lawmakers legislated
minimum standards to regulate work hours, housing, and factories. Once laws
required shorter work hours and a minimum age for child labor, educators
forced schools to change. Educational changes stimulated a variety of other

reform activities among other disenfranchised groups of people such as women and ethnic minorities. This reform activity eventually led to women's right to vote and to anti-discrimination laws in colleges and universities, in the work place, and in housing. Other reform activity centered around clothing, food, alcohol, and drug issues, including the temperance movement, which instigated Prohibition. People in the free love movement, begun in the 1870s, worked to counter oppressive marriage laws; leaders of this reform group even advocated sex education in the schools. Advocates of one kind of reform often participated in other related causes. For instance, some men and women in the free love movement also spoke out against corsets and pointed toe shoes. In the late nineteenth and early twentieth century troubling social needs stimulated momentous political and social reforms which eventually brought about great change in people's lives.

How working people used time in their daily lives changed. People began to have leisure time, and many creative spokespeople for ideal forms of recreation preached about how to fill this time in useful ways. Church leaders, who preached about proper use of leisure time, encouraged, organized, and sponsored team sports, both to save the souls of their parishioners and attract more members. Their movement gained the affectionate title of "muscular Christianity." Historians of popular culture Golby and Purdue, (1985), refer to a gentleman called Charles Kingsley who spoke about muscular Christianity in England. Page Smith refers to this phenomenon in America as does Foster Rhea Dulles, (1965). Leisure time, the advocates preached, could be spent frivolously in cheap entertainments which often led to drinking, brawling, and promiscuity, or could be filled fruitfully with elevating pastimes which enlighten, enrich, and educate, thereby, achieving the goal of bettering oneself. Sports activity became associated with healthy, clean living. Golby and Purdue label this message "rational recreation." Churches and labor unions organized numerous clubs which sponsored lectures, classes, and other educational activities at their meetings. The Chautauqua movement epitomized this educational type of recreation in the United States.

Other institutions besides churches and educational institutions housed recreation and social reform activities. In the United States, social worker and educator Jane Addams established the first settlement house in Chicago and trained others who set up more settlement houses in other cities. These became centers for recreational, social, educational, and political activities to help the local working poor and integrate the large numbers of immigrants into American society. In addition to social service specialists, a wide variety of other experts praised the benefits of new forms of self-improvement, including physical activity of all kinds: swimming, hiking, games, sports, and dancing. Settlement houses sponsored pageants, sports activities, and a variety of classes. Among those offered were some of the earliest "natural" dance classes. The call for improvement went beyond the personal to the care and improvement of the natural environment, urban and rural. The goals of physical well-being of people and care for nature coalesced in the back-to-nature movement, which brought about forest and wildlife preservation, animal and nature study clubs for adults and children, and the playground movement. Boy Scouts and Girl Scouts, Campfire Girls, and other nature study and service-centered organizations started at this time. Public and recreational activity, in turn, stimulated educational changes in the form of physical education classes, nature study in elementary classrooms, science classes in high schools, and field trips for all.

The efforts of people in progressive social movements and the back-to-nature movement helped establish municipal, national, and state parks, and protected large areas of wilderness from residential or commercial use. Helen Moller describes the ideal environment for dance as an outdoor setting similar to Arcadia. Arcady, the poetic form of Arcadia, is "a mountainous region of ancient Greece, traditionally known for the contented pastoral innocence of its people" (Stein, 1983:76). Historian Peter Schmitt, in *Back to Nature: The Arcadian Myth in Urban America* (1969), distinguishes "Arcadian" idealism from "agrarianism." In both, people responded to the stresses, problems, and evils of urban living. They differ, however, in that an agrarian idealist wants to go back to the land and values it for economic reasons, while the Arcadian idealist espouses a return to nature for spiritual reasons. The idealization of nature, as a theme, runs through many of the books of the dancer-writers.

Educational and Artistic Contexts

In every era, William Fleming points out in *Art, Music and Ideas* (1970), Europeans, and then Americans, have turned to ancient Greece for inspiration to solve contemporary problems. The renewed study of ancient Greece which inspired the educational and artistic reforms at the turn of this century began two centuries before with the excavations of Herculaneum in 1709 and Pompeii in 1748. Scholars not only studied the archaeological evidence of ancient daily living but these discoveries also stimulated renewed examination of the historical documents written during the classical period of ancient Greece and Rome.

The recovered artifacts clarified the reality of ancient living and enabled experts to revise their interpretations of history, separating fact from fiction, speculation from practice. After the nineteenth-century democratic revolutions, between the 1870s and the 1920s, leaders in architecture, literature, higher education, and sports again turned to ancient Greece as a model for solutions to the problems of developing democratic nation-states and to counter the negative impact of the Industrial Revolution.

Several of our writers—Helen Moller, Margaret H'Doubler, Isadora and Raymond Duncan—numbered among the many people enamored with idealized Greek culture. In his discussion of Isadora and Raymond Duncan, Victor Seroff in *The Real Isadora* (1971), suggests why: some of the Duncans' understanding of ancient Greek culture "stemmed from a general American interest in (and version of!) an ancient culture, resulting at that time in many a popular lecture series from many a highbrow podium in which Americans tended to congratulate themselves as direct heirs of Athenian democracy and its attendant arts" (Seroff, 1971:55). Isadora and Raymond Duncan, relates Seroff, had a more informed understanding of Greek culture as a result of their study of Greek art in museums and books. Even so, their view of Greece, he contends, blended the popular version with their particular selection of "genuine" Greek culture.

Although artists looked to ancient Greece for a model to integrate the arts, in America, a nationalist movement emerged which supported original American art not derived from or dependent on European schools or styles. Isadora Duncan's ideas for creating an American dance reflect the artistic revolution which began at the turn of the century. She was a young artist in the United States when a number of American painters, writers, and musicians challenged the tradition of following European standards of art. Robert Henri, a friend of Isadora, led the "Ash-can" school of painters—Arthur Bowen Davies, George Luks, William Glackens, John Sloan, and lithographer George Bellows—in their first exhibition of uniquely American painting and prints. Photographers Alfred Stieglitz, Edward Steichen, Lewis Hickes Hines; architect Frank Lloyd Wright; film-maker David W. Griffith; novelists Theodore Dreiser, Upton Sinclair, Jack London, Sherwood Anderson, Sinclair Lewis, Willa Cather, Edith Wharton; short story writers O. Henry, Alice Dunbar-Nelson; poets Ezra Pound, Vachel Lindsay, Robert Frost, Edgar Lee Masters, Edwin Robinson, Hilda Doolittle (H.D.); composers Arthur Farwell, Theodore Chanler, Irving Berlin—all contributed to the blossoming of American arts at this time.

In the late 1800s, the oppressive social conditions which resulted from the destructive results of industrialization on people and nature propelled an artistic revolution in Europe and the United States. The thinkers and artists caught up in this revolution abhorred the enormous economic and social inequities which caused great suffering among several strata of the population. Many artists, writers, and musicians rebelled against the official academies which set the standards for and limited the subject matter of their arts. They sought new techniques and subjects for which they received no instruction in the established schools. Many artists turned to the ideas of radical political thinkers of the time who offered egalitarian solutions to the social and economic dilemmas which produced their artistic dissatisfaction: Karl Marx, Robert Owen, Charles Fourier. Political observers variously called the movements these and others led: "radical," "utopian," "socialist," "anarchist." Though their means of bringing about changes differed, the theorists agreed on some basic principles to help humanity escape from the inequities and artificialities created by industry and academies: they warned against the hollowness of materialism, they advocated shared wealth, they stood for individual freedom and autonomy, they envisioned community-based living, and they urged the populace to challenge the status quo.

The arts and artists play a central role in the social radicals' schemes of social and economic salvation. The arts, they taught, can serve not merely to entertain the wealthy bourgeois as they had done in the past, but now they must reach the common people, the masses, and give them access to beauty, freedom, and spiritual harmony. This attitude toward the function of art rejects the countervailing idea of "art for art's sake," advocated by some artists. Many of the most innovative artists of this time identified with socialist, anarchist, or utopian political movements organized by followers of these social and economic theorists. For instance, the proclaimed philosophic and spiritual guides of Isadora Duncan—William Blake, Walt Whitman, Richard Wagner, and Friedrich Nietzsche—in differing ways, all espoused this kind of radical utopian thinking.

Concerned people founded philosophic and religious movements which reflected this utopian vision and the role of art in life. These movements evolved from Romanticism: back to nature, idealized peasant life, tragedy as part of life, and the struggle for freedom. Ralph Waldo Emerson and Henry David Thoreau popularized one such movement, Transcendentalism, in the United States. Transcendentalists view the world as a unified whole; they see human, plant, animal, and non-living matter as connected, interrelated, and interdependent. Transcendentalism contributed to the more diffuse spiritualism. Spiritualists believe a soul, a spirit, or a unique radiating essence exists in all matter. These ideas became more formalized in the Theosophical Society to which Raymond

Duncan belonged. This aesthetic universalism took root in education. In Jean-Jacques Rousseau's educational theory, children gain understanding of themselves and civilization through doing and participating in art experiences; this central tenant of Rousseau's thinking influenced school reformers. The ideas of many of the dancer-writers I study here reflect these radical political, social, artistic, and educational trends (Egbert, 1970).

Pressure for changes in education came from many interested parties, not just people advocating Rousseau's theories. Progressive politicians, advocates of women's rights, social workers, philosophers, military leaders, African-Americans, educators, and members of the newly evolved profession of psychologists numbered among the experts who advocated educational reform (See Mayer, 1964; Gutek, 1986; Wingo, 1974). Throughout most of the nineteenth-century, though more children—boys and girls—attended and remained longer in schools than ever before in history, teachers in schools in Europe and America continued to teach the same subjects: reading, writing, spelling, arithmetic, geography, ancient history, grammar, Latin, and Greek, using traditional methods of memorization and recitation. Discipline was strict, often corporal, and teachers insisted that children sit still and be quiet. Educational reform takes a long time, but Progressive education reformers changed teaching methods—classes became more child-centered than subject-centered—and they introduced new subject matter—the arts, sciences, social studies, and physical education including games and folk dancing.

Reform in education changed the method of instruction as well as the subject matter. In the second half of the nineteenth century, if children took part in any physical exercise they practiced some form of gymnastics, usually based on the systems evolved from military training. G. Stanley Hall, an educational psychologist, taught and wrote influential books on educational reform. In his two-volume *Educational Problems* (1911), Hall devotes a long chapter to "The Educational Value of Dancing and Pantomime," in which he advocates creative dance for all children to develop their motor, emotional, and imaginative abilities. Hall described dancing "as the liberal, humanistic culture of emotions by motions" (Hall, 1911:42). Hall influenced other well-known progressive educational reformers, among them Francis Parker and John Dewey. Parker and later Dewey set up experimental elementary schools in the United States where the arts played an integral and vital part of children's learning. Changes in the schools, in turn, stimulated improvements in teacher-training institutes, called Normal Schools, and invigorated the scientific study of children and adolescents. The entire field of education gained prestige in public opinion and legitimacy in the academic realm. Proper education, reformers thought, could solve the major problems of society (Rushdoony, 1963).

At the turn of the twentieth century, many people, including artists, worked to shift political and social power in society from the old aristocratic class, the industrial "robber barons," and military leaders into the hands of the middle class. At that time the broad definition of the middle class often included everyone except the non-working poor. Artists joined the groups of people advocating these changes; reciprocally, these increasingly democratic social changes stimulated their work. Most of the innovations in each art came from artists deeply influenced by radical utopian social ideals and political goals proposed by thinkers who dreamed about equalizing the rich and poor, the powerful and powerless, the weak and strong. Frequently the dancer-writers analyzed here advocate "free" dance as a way to achieve similar utopian ideals. Their goals reflect those of the rational recreationists who thought that working people would benefit from the enjoyment of the fine arts. The more beauty the workers saw, believed the reformers, the more they would seek to apply that ideal to other areas in their lives, and, perhaps, they would be saved from such evils as drinking and gambling. Stated in Freudian terms, art expression (or sports, swimming, or hiking) allowed people to release their repressed emotions in constructive ways.

Dancing

In most economic and social classes in Europe and the United States, people enjoyed ballroom, folk, or "play-party" (square or round) dancing for recreation. Even in the early part of the nineteenth century dance teachers taught these kinds of social recreational dances in cities and towns in private and public schools, colleges, and in private studios. As early as 1817 cadets at West Point learned ballroom dances during their summer encampment for their morale and their deportment (Kraus and Chapman, 1981:112). Dance teachers published many instruction books of the popular dances they taught to their students. Throughout the history of European theater dance, especially during and after the Romantic period of the 1830s and 1840s, these recreational forms of folk or national dancing provided source material for ballet choreographers in Europe and America. Dancing as social and recreational activity continued among people of all classes as a participatory pastime and as an enjoyable form of entertainment in many venues.

Dancing did not rank among the redeeming activities recommended by the high-minded reformers. They associated it with lower class entertainment in pubs, drinking rooms, and music halls, and thus condemned it out of hand as leading to vice. This association caused some early modern dance artists to detest jazz music and dance. Other reformers associated dancing with the upper-class "fine art" of ballet which continued as part of opera and therefore remained out of reach of the middle class. As an activity in which to participate, only people who wanted to become professional dancers considered ballet.

During this period, the academic discipline of dance had not yet been defined clearly. Few traditional scholars recognized that a body of knowledge about dance existed; they did not consider it a field separate from music or theater. Anyone looking for information about the history of dance, for instance, would look in the back of books about music or theater to find a summary of the main events. Yet for hundreds of years, a few scholars and dance devotees from many disciplines, including dance itself, had been researching and writing about dance and dancing. In 1929 Cyril Beaumont published his *Bibliography of Dancing*, listing entries in alphabetical order by author. In his *Bibliography of Dancing* (1936), Paul D. Magriel helped to define the body of knowledge for dance by categorizing dance books in the following manner:

1. General Works
2. History and Criticism of Dance
3. Folk, National, Regional, and Ethnological Dances, with entries for all the continents and major groups of islands
4. The Art of Dancing
5. Ballet
6. Mime and Pantomime
7. Masques
8. Accessories

Magriel lists most of the books analyzed in the present study in categories of General Works, History and Criticism of the Dance, and The Art of Dancing. He does not list the book by Beegle and Crawford.

Magriel evolved his own method of categorizing dance books because the most commonly used system for classification of books on dance and the other arts, the system devised in 1876 by Melvil Dewey, he found unsatisfactory and woefully inadequate. Dewey's system divides the world's books into ten areas. 700 is the section for the fine arts (general), and it includes:

710 Landscape and civic art;

720 Architecture;
730 Sculpture; Plastic arts;
740 Drawing, Decoration, Design;
750 Painting;
760 Engraving;
770 Photography;
780 Music;
790 Amusements.

Dewey categorized Dancing under, 790 Amusements, in 793 Indoor entertainment, parties. The category reads: ".3 Dancing, .32 Artistic Dancing." Thus,
dancing ranks as a subsidiary within a non-artistic category and is of tertiary
importance paralleling Mausoleums, Bricabrac, Fanciwork, and Photozincografy
in Dewey's category "Engraving." Dewey not only disliked dancing; he tucked
Opera away in Theater, 792, as ".4 Opera, Lyric Drama, .5 Comic opera, and .6
Operetta and musical comedy." Though more flexible than the Dewey system,
the book classification system used by the Library of Congress incorporates a
prejudice similar to Dewey's. It also places dance in a small category with call
numbers GV 1580 to GV 1799 and separates some areas of dance, such as dance
therapy and dance in religion, from the main section for dance (Munro,
1967:219-230). This system sandwiches dance between magic and circus and
thus perpetuates Dewey's view of dance as an amusement.

The ideas of the dancer-writers I examine reflect the political, social,
educational, and artistic changes occurring during the first third of the twentieth
century. They couch their words in the terms utilized by the reformers in their
various movements. Seen in this complex and multi-layered context, their ideas
make sense, as does the history of modern dance which followed in the 1930s
and 1940s. But that is getting ahead of the story. Before analyzing the ideas of
these seven dancer-writers, an introduction to them and their books is in order.

2

The Dancer-Writers and Their Books

Who were these dancers who wrote books about dancing in the early twentieth century? What was the nature of their writing? Why did they write? To whom did they address their messages? This chapter begins to answer these questions, offers background about the authors and their books, and introduces their writing about dancing published in the first thirty years of this century. Because I found only limited information about some of these dancer-writers, the length of my account about each differs considerably.

Isadora Duncan

Because of her outstanding performing career as a dancer and choreographer, Isadora Duncan (1877-1927) stands as the most renowned of all the modern dance pioneers discussed here. She achieved fame as a dancer of her own form of free dance, having rejected the strictures of ballet: its traditional costume, its prescribed technique, its programmatic music, and its fairytale subject matter. Widely acclaimed in the Western world during the first twenty-five years of this century, she toured Europe, the United States, and Russia; and she established schools, first near Berlin and later in Paris and Moscow, to teach her system of free dance. By the 1930s the kind of dancing she composed and performed became known as "modern" dance.

Though scholars acknowledge Isadora Duncan, the "barefoot dancer," as a major pioneer of early American modern dance, they less often recognize her for her theoretical contributions to the field of dance. John Martin, in *America Dancing* (1936), credits Duncan with establishing the theoretical basis for this century's major innovative dance form, modern dance. She asked the central questions about composing dances, Martin claims; these questions engaged the many dancers and choreographers who followed her lead in challenging the traditional dance forms at the turn of this century. Duncan often lectured before or after her concerts and regularly wrote her ideas about dancing in essays published in her programs. She never organized these writings in a coherent way.

In 1928, soon after Isadora Duncan's tragic death the year before, Sheldon Cheney, theater historian and editor of *Theatre Arts Monthly*, collected her writings as well as drawings and photographs of Isadora into a book, *The Art of the Dance.* In his introduction Cheney explains how Isadora edited and reworked some of her essays. She wrote for a variety of uses: in her concert programs, her autobiography, *My Life* (1927), letters, articles, and foreign-language interviews. He carefully edited the different versions from several languages and printed them in a rough chronological order. This collection of the writing by Isadora Duncan serves as the source of my analysis of her thinking about dance.

Isadora wrote her essays over a span of more than twenty years. She writes in the didactic and inspirational writing style common to many late nineteenth-century writers. She uses reverential metaphors and poetic generalizations, and often relies on florid word choice. Throughout the analysis of her ideas, I have simplified her words and paraphrased her ideas in language more familiar to readers of today.

Raymond Duncan

Though dance historians habitually discuss the contributions to dance history of Isadora Duncan they rarely include her older brother in their analysis of this formative period of dance history. Isadora Duncan's biographers acknowledge that Raymond Duncan (1874-1966), dancer, teacher, and choreographer, became famous for his devotion to Greek civilization. In 1914, for a conference at his Dance Academy in Paris, he published an essay in French entitled, "La Danse et la Gymnastique." Because the work of Isadora attracts so much attention, few researchers have examined the contribution of Raymond to dance thinking. Lillian Loewenthal in *The Search for Isadora: The Legend and Legacy of Isadora Duncan* (1993) devotes a chapter to the life and work of Raymond. He lived his belief in the value of ancient and contemporary rural Greek ways of working, crafting, and dancing. Though a gifted and moving performer in his own right, his teaching had considerable influence; among his more well known students, Margaret Morris established a school of natural dance in England and developed Raymond Duncan's dancing techniques. I analyze the ideas contained in his essay "Dance and Gymnastic" in this book.

Raymond Duncan focuses his essay on the aesthetic qualities of properly executed gymnastic exercises which he devised. He places his ideas about dance in a larger context which reflects a unified vision of humankind, animals, and nature in the universe; the life-style of the Greek people in their mountain villages exemplifies this unified vision of the ideal life. Though he titles his essay "Dance and Gymnastics," both gymnastic and dance become metaphors for life. Duncan's essay, the only pamphlet analyzed here, does not have photographs.

Mary Beegle

Because rigorous and systematic research in dance is a recent phenomenon, today's dance scholars have almost unlimited opportunities to fill gaps in our knowledge of dance history and theory. Recently, Naima Prevots in her book, *American Pageantry: A Movement for Art and Democracy* (1990) filled one of those gaps about the beginnings of university-level modern dance. In her chapter on dance, Prevots introduces Mary Beegle and describes her work as a teacher of "natural dance" in pageantry courses at Columbia Teachers College, Barnard College, and Dartmouth College Summer School. Before teaching with Crawford, Beegle studied dance and pageantry in Europe. After returning from Europe she received her B.S. from Columbia University and a Diploma from the Chalif Russian Normal School of Dancing, a respected center for ballet training, in 1910. Beegle's writing and teaching, through her students and colleagues, such as dance educators Gertrude Colby, Margaret H'Doubler, and Bird Larson, profoundly influenced the history of dance education.

Prevots describes Beegle and Crawford's *Community Drama and Pageantry* (1916) as one of the most thorough pageantry books written during the pageantry movement, 1910-1922. Her co-author Jack Randall Crawford, a drama professor, held a position at Yale University, whose press published their book. Together, he and Beegle taught pageantry courses in summer programs at Dartmouth College and elsewhere when pageantry reached its height. Influential colleges and universities around the country, Prevots discovered, frequently used their book as a text in pageantry courses; for instance, pageantry teachers used it at University of California-Los Angeles as early as 1917, at the University of Wisconsin in 1918, at the University of California-Berkeley in 1923, and at the University of Southern California in 1924 (Prevots, 1990: 136-138). Because of the strong dance component in these courses, after the pageantry movement faded dance teachers developed autonomous dance programs and departments such as the one Margaret H'Doubler established.

A pageant, Beegle and Crawford explain in the body of their book, as a spectacle, must please the eye; it usually occurs outdoors and dance blends with the other arts into the total organic pageant production. To achieve this visual aim, the three fundamental principles which govern any dramatic production—sound, light, and movement—must be used effectively. Beegle and Crawford place dance into the broad category of "movement," along with gesture, acting, and grouping. Dance and song, as integral parts of a pageant's dramatic entity, function to connect, deepen, and develop the events of the main story or plot in interludes and pictorial episodes.

The two-part chapter and extensive bibliography on dance, probably written by Beegle, contains theoretical and practical information which applies today as it did in the first quarter of this century. In Part I of chapter 9, "The Dance" (pp. 190-216), Beegle defines dance as "natural dancing," explains its function, and then offers principles of dance composition and dance technique. Beegle published her ideas about "natural" dance five years before Margaret H'Doubler advocated "natural dancing" in her book, *A Manual of Dancing* (1921), and eight years before Gertrude Colby wrote *Natural Rhythms and Dances* (1924) in which she advocates "natural dancing." Part II of Beegle's chapter on dance, "Rehearsal and Training" (pp. 219-233), contains guidelines for teaching natural dancing and offers practical rehearsal instructions for group and solo dancers in a pageant. Reflecting her extensive experience with teaching and choreographing natural dance Beegle wrote her guidelines and instructions authoritatively in a clear and concise manner.

Beegle's ideas show the influence of the famous Swiss music educator Emile Jaques-Dalcroze. In the bibliography on dance she adds a special annotation about the value of his work for dancers. Prevots surmises that Beegle probably studied with Jaques-Dalcroze in Europe in the early 1900s or his students in New York, before she taught at Columbia Teachers College. Beegle's definition of dance as "creative self-expression through the interpretation of ideas through rhythmic movement," compares closely with Jaques-Dalcroze's: "Dancing is the art of expressing emotion by means of rhythmic bodily movement" (Jaques-Dalcroze, 1912:232). Beegle substitutes "ideas" (derived from moods which express emotion) for Jaques-Dalcroze's "emotion."

Helen Moller

Unlike Beegle, who taught in colleges and universities, Helen Moller directed The Temple, a private school of Natural Dancing in the New York City area in the early twentieth century. Elizabeth Kendall listed her as an "aesthetic type" of California girl who toured the top circuits in a vaudeville dancing act in 1917. No other biographical information about Helen Moller is easily available. I could find no entry about her in any Who's Who or biographical index. Standard book catalogues do not give her birth and death dates. Her married name was Mrs. Robert Poole. A reporter called her "the American priestess of the dance" in *The Toledo Times* which carried an ad for her school on 5 March 1916. The text describes the picture shown: "The figure shows a camera silhouette fixing for deliberate study the correct poise of the arms and hands to express admiration of a growing plant in flower" (*The Toledo Times*, 1916). The photograph pictures a barefoot and bare-armed young woman, dressed in a transparent Greek style tunic, holding a long-stem rose in her left hand, while her right arm is gracefully curved above the flower. The young woman tilts her head slightly to the left, balances her body weight on the balls of her feet with her heels a few inches off the floor, and places her right foot slightly ahead of the left. A short report in *Vanity Fair* describes Miss Moller's school of natural dancing as especially successful and efficient in its outdoor classes. One of the many schools of natural dancing, hers had recently appeared: the number "seems to have quadrupled during the past year." Miss Moller's girls range in age from sixteen to twenty-five and come from five countries in Europe and America (*Vanity Fair*, 19 July 1916). She gave concerts with her ensemble. A program announcement for 11 March at 3 P.M. (no year) lists the composers of the music to be performed for "sincere lovers of music and interpretive dancing: Gluck, Tarnefeldt, Grieg, Rachmaninoff, Strauss, Brams [sic], Dvorak, Kreisler, Sibelius, Ilynsky, Sousa."

The book review of Moller's book, *Dancing with Helen Moller* (1918), published in *Book Review Digest* (1918) introduces the focus and style of her teachings:

> Helen Moller's own "statement of her philosophy and practice and teaching formed upon the classic Greek model, and adapted to meet the aesthetic and hygienic needs of today," (subtitle) supplemented by 43 full page plates of her dancing pupils and an introduction by Ivan Narodny author of "The Dance."

> This book is indeed a "new message of beauty to modern civilization." Dancing is regarded not merely as a desirable accomplishment but as a means of expressing the soul and acquiring that rhythmic harmony in the body that makes for higher health and happiness. Music is a constantly enriching inspiration to dancing; and dancing, music's twin sister, affords us creative interpretation of the latter as well as also of that more silent art, poetry. This book — as Miss Moller desires — inspires one to be an active enemy of all that is false and ugly and a practicing advocate of whatever is true and beautiful.

> If the reader expects to find a poetic plea combined with good practical common-sense to become a worshiper of Terpsichore, he will not be disappointed. (Reely, 1918:312)

Moller defines dancing as a "state of mind acting upon the emotions and producing physical expression" (Moller, 1918:19). This unity of mind, emotions, and physical expression emerges as one of Moller's main themes. In her introductory chapter, Moller explains the focus of her book. She is not writing a history book, because traditional dance history books, she claims, focus mainly on dances which appear on theater stages. Her book concerns the activity of dancing which is a "natural gift provided for the pleasure and benefit of all humanity" (Moller, 1918:21). Except at the end of each of her six essays, she alternates her written text with full-page photographs. The captions and the photographs provide the reader with a survey of the techniques and style of composition she teaches in her school. Also in these captions she uniformly identifies the emotion which generates the physical expression.

Eleanor Elder

Compared to Moller's book, Eleanor Elder's *Dance, A National Art* (1918), a 28-page book with eight photographs, seems little more than a pamphlet. It contains several layers of information about this period in modern dance history. To start, it provides a detailed connection between Raymond Duncan's technique and that of Margaret Morris. In addition, Elder's historical information, descriptive notes, and theoretical ideas link Raymond Duncan's role in early modern dance to Isadora Duncan's dancing; Helen Moller's techniques and ideals to Margaret Morris and the Duncan siblings; and the Duncans' style of natural Greek dancing to the teachings of Mary Beegle and Margaret H'Doubler. Though Elder's essay touches on many topics basic to dance theory, she focuses on the educational value of physical expression, especially taught through the natural dancing techniques evolved by Raymond Duncan. Elder explains the six fundamental positions of Raymond's system, the "laws" that govern them, and provides photographs and stick-figure drawings of these positions. She also pictures a group of adults studying natural dancing in India who have applied these techniques to express their response to a poem. Approximately half the book contains educational theory and dance history, while the other half describes practice.

Eleanor Elder, whom Margaret Morris mentions twice in her autobiography, played a leading role in a 1913 production of "Snow White and the Seven Little Dwarfs" and started Morris's first travelling theater soon after that production. She had a long association with Morris. In 1958, Elder served as one of three vice presidents of the Organizing Committee for the Fiftieth Anniversary of the Margaret Morris Movement, as Morris called the technique system she devised.

The most detailed information in Elder's little book concerns the work of Morris and the importance of Raymond Duncan's six fundamental positions. Elder identifies Morris as an artist who carries the fire of innovation from the past into the future. She incorporates detail about Morris that Morris does not even mention in her autobiography: her appearance dancing in a church as a small girl, her extensive ballet training, and her decision to leave her ballet master to study with Raymond Duncan and then teach his method of natural dancing. Elder describes Morris's first triumph in teaching her Greek dancing to poor children in London. Elder puts this style of dance teaching into a broader context when she reports: "There are many schools of dancing that are turning out graceful, healthy pupils, but none of them produce one quarter of the originality on the part of the pupils themselves, as this school in Chelsea does" (Elder, 1918:11). Teachers, she explains, in many of these schools appear to have reacted against the rigid Victorian teaching methods by allowing the dance students excessive freedom, whereas the students of Morris show discipline and meet the highest standards of technique and performance.

Writing at the end of World War I, Elder suggests that that historical moment offers an exceptional opportunity for educators to make much needed changes in the physical side of education. As evidence of this need, she points to the bent, tense, and inactive bodies of many people in the British population. Educational dancing, she believes, can correct this problem. This creative and natural type of dancing contrasts with the kind of theater dancing taught for professional training which creates abnormal development of muscles.

Margaret H'Doubler

Like Beegle, Margaret H'Doubler taught in a university setting. Dance students may be familiar with her most evolved ideas because her book, *Dance: A Creative Art Experience,* written in 1940, continues to be assigned in dance classes in many university dance programs. The ideas in her first two books, *A Manual for Dancing* (1921; MD), and *Dance and Its Place in Education* (1925; DPE), analyzed here, are much less widely known. H'Doubler's ideas about the educational value of dance, its rhythmic basis, and the purpose of technique, composition, and performance show continuity throughout her career. Her ideas, especially in these early books, also reflect those of her teacher and colleague Mary Beegle and the philosophy of progressive educators and rational recreationists who wanted to elevate the tastes of their students to appreciate the finer things in life.

H'Doubler wrote her first two books to "help better teaching of dance in schools and colleges" (DPE, 1925:viii). The major portion of both provides readers with detailed verbal and pictorial (drawings) instructions of "movement fundamentals," her substitute for gymnastic exercises or ballet technique. They fill one-half of *A Manual for Dancing* and one-third of *Dance and Its Place in Education. A Manual for Dancing,* a text for her classes, she self-published. Of its total of 106 pages it contains 31 empty pages for "memorandum" to be used by her students for taking notes. Harcourt, Brace and Company published her much longer second book (283 pages) which ends with an unpaginated performance program of one of her student concerts. In her second book, H'Doubler deepens the theoretical ideas she introduces in the five-page Section One of her first little book. Her educator's emphasis on creative movement instruction for self-expression is evident in these early books.

Compared to most of the other dancer-writers discussed in the present work, H'Doubler writes a thorough theoretical analysis of dance. She includes the materials of dance: the body, the senses and the kinesthetic sense, everyday movement and dance movement. Of the elements of movement—time, space and force—she only discusses time. About the processes of dancing, she covers technique, composition, use of the other arts, and performance. Dance, as an entity, does not concern her. She focuses on students dancing, and on the teacher's role, and occasionally touches on the audience viewpoint. She high-lights the functions of dancing in an historical and cultural context but concentrates mostly on the educational issues and values of interpretive dancing.

Margaret Morris

The following entry from *The Encyclopedia of Dance and Ballet* (1977) summar-izes the contributions to dance of Margaret Morris:

> Morris, Margaret, b. London, 1891, (d. 1980). English dancer and movement theorist. She founded her own school in 1910 in London and was a pioneer in the teaching of free dance. In 1925, founded the Margaret Morris Movement (still extant) and devised a system of notation. In 1947 founded her short-lived Celtic Ballet in Glasgow. An influential figure, she published several books including her autobiography, *My Life in Movement* (London 1969). (Clarke and Vaughn, 1977:241)

This entry barely introduces her, for her pioneering efforts, in many ways, equalled the contributions of American modern dance pioneers Ruth St. Denis and Ted Shawn. Both Morris and Denishawn established schools (Denishawn in 1915), innovated methods of composition, taught influential dancers, actors, and choreographers, and wrote several books which provide detailed information about the development of free dance in the first quarter of this century. Morris's interests went beyond theater dance; the movement system she devised led her to work with athletes, pregnant women, and handicapped children in England and Europe. In her school in London (which moved several times) she established a public forum as a meeting place for artists and intellectuals and a theater for her performances and others. She saw the necessity of, and then devised, a movement notation system. In her school curriculum, she offered classes in art, music, set and costume design, lighting, and stage managing. Her pioneer work in free dance and dance education deserves more attention than it has thus far received.

Morris wrote *Margaret Morris Dancing* (1926), with 40 photographs by artist and photographer Fred Daniels, to disseminate her ideas and her movement system. Four of the seven chapters in this book appeared in another form in other publications:

Chapter 1, "Health and Physical Exercises" in *The Daily Sketch*, 23 June 1919

Chapter 2, "Movement, Colour, and Sound in Education" in *The New Era,* July 1922;

Chapter 5, "Theatrical Production: Designing, Acting and Dancing for the Stage" in *Theatrecraft* (she gives no date);

Chapter 6, "My Notation System" in *Daily Chronicle*, 5 December 1913.

In her last chapter, "My Past in Dancing, and My Training of the Dancers of the Future," Morris credits her teachers for their contribution to her concepts of free-dance training. She studied ballet with John D'Auban and is grateful to him for being tolerant of innovation within the traditional ballet system he taught. The only other teacher she credits is Raymond Duncan: "It was Raymond Duncan who first made me realize the latent possibilities in dancing, by starting from a simple and natural technique instead of a purely artificial one, hampered by endless conventions" (Morris, 1926:84).

Though Raymond Duncan's exercises stimulated her movement system and she incorporates them into her own, Morris differentiates her work from his because she is "more interested in the construction of a new and living form of dance" (Morris, 1926: 85). She articulates the educational principles of her new "living form" of dance in *Margaret Morris Dancing* (1926). Her ideas about the relationship between music and dance also reflect those taught and written by

Emile Jaques-Dalcroze, the famous music professor who taught his *gymnastique rhythmique* to musicians, dancers, and actors in his Institute for Applied Rhythm in Hellerau, Switzerland, established in 1911.

These seven dancer-writers—Isadora Duncan, Raymond Duncan, Mary Beegle, Helen Moller, Eleanor Elder, Margaret H'Doubler, and Margaret Morris— have much in common. They all wrote books or pamphlets to explain their ideas about dancing. They all evolved technique systems to develop their students' dancing ability. And they were all educators. Isadora and Raymond Duncan, Helen Moller and Margaret Morris established private schools. Eleanor Elder taught in Morris's school, while Mary Beegle and Margaret H'Doubler taught in college or university settings.

As will become evident in succeeding chapters, these dancer-writers also share basic ideas about the nature of the body and movement; the role of technique for dancing; the central power of rhythm in dancing, art, and life; and the influence of classical Greece on dancing. In each chapter I will present the material in approximately chronological order. I begin with information about and concepts of Isadora Duncan because her contemporaries share many of her ideas. Though they agree with Isadora, their careers all began during the first third of the twentieth century. Similar cultural pressures and aesthetic values influenced them; thus they may be regarded as compatriots in the artistic development of early modern dance rather than followers or imitators of a leader.

3
Dancing in its
Social and Historical Contexts

This examination of the ideas found in the books by the dancer-writers begins with a look at how their conceptualization of the social and historical context of Western dance clarifies their ideas about the body, everyday movement, dance movement, composition, performance, and the relationship of dance with the other arts. A surprisingly unified picture of dancing emerges from the writings. They agree more frequently than they disagree about the meaning, components, goals, and benefits of the newly emerging form of dancing. As in other areas, the influence of Isadora Duncan is evident.

In a few of her essays, Isadora discusses the cultural context in which dancing and dance-making occur. To be an art, she insists, dance must speak for our times; it must externalize our emotions, and emerge from our lives (Duncan, 1928:139). The contemporary dance must balance the strained and awkward manner of people's daily movements. Even contemporary clothing, she complains, prevents people from breathing freely (Duncan, 1928:100). In contrast with the current restrictions, she refers to Greek times, when, even before Aeschylus, people danced together to express collective emotions such as grief, aggression, or joy. This expression became the dance of the Greek chorus. By the time of Sophocles, she points out, the arts were united: dancing, poetry, music, dramaturgy, and architecture formed a single art in Greek theater. She traces this ideal of unifying the arts to Wagner's music dramas many centuries later; she too wants to achieve this unity in her dance art of the early twentieth century.

In her discussion of the cultural context of dance Isadora explains why she rejects ballet. Like other dance forms and dances from other cultures and eras, ballet does not fit our times. It grew out of the falseness and shallowness of the most polluted seventeenth and eighteenth-century courts and suits that time (Duncan, 1928:73). The sickly sentimental and romantic Mazurka and Waltz of the nineteenth century, Isadora claims, do not suit modern times (Duncan, 1928:50). She repeatedly criticizes jazz; she regards it as obscene, reflecting the sexual puritanism of the radical utopians. Though jazz fits the needs of "South Africans" for whom it is natural (Duncan, 1928:49), she believes it does not fit the American people. The freely moving pelvis in jazz does not express the emotional or spiritual ideas she wants to convey in dance. Other dancers share Isadora's rejection of popular "negro" dances and even dance critic John Martin shows this bias in his early writing. They associate jazz dance with juke-joint dancing and with breaking the laws of Prohibition. Isadora's obvious anti-African-American feelings reflect the common late-Victorian racist attitude toward non-Caucasian people which sociologists and geneticists couched in respectable scientific language. Between 1912 and 1930, claims Stanley Coben, academicians helped repudiate the scientific rationale for racism, although many people have continued to pre-judge those from other cultures in a stereotypic and hierarchical manner. Isadora's views evince an elite perspective which denigrate popular arts and the people who create them.

Though Isadora's writing centers on the role of dance as art, she considers the religious, social, and recreational functions of dance in human society. She acknowledges that dance always played a vital part in human religion (Duncan, 1928:132). It still plays a central role in courtship, but, she claims, the sterile and futile social dances of today show the peoples' need for expressive dancing (Duncan, 1928: 125). She decries the forms of entertainment dance, such as burlesque and skirt dancing, used for amusement or exhibition where audience members come to have their senses titillated (Duncan, 1928:120). For dance to be understood as an art, it must be considered as sacred, not profane (Duncan, 1928:122). This dichotomy of sacred versus profane reflects her Delsartian (See Chapter 6 below) background and her romantic idealism. The extreme terms with which she discusses dance stem from the social and cultural context in which she lived and created. Dance, she believes, must be recognized not only for its social and entertainment values, but as an art.

Raymond Duncan's essay reflects the utopian vision of the back-to-nature movement intertwined with an idealized concept of peasant Greek life. He describes the shepherds in Epirus, a mountain village near where he and the other Duncans tried to build a grand temple of the dance in 1903. He invites his readers to join the shepherds around a campfire to gaze into the starry night or walk under a blazing sun, which can be seen against a blue sky with snow-capped Pindus mountains in the distance. This experience, he contends, cannot be translated into words but can be expressed in harmonious dance movement.

In his final summary, Raymond integrates song, music, and intellectual discourse, and contends that they can express life if they are done by means of true dance.

Imagine that we might succeed in introducing the true dance in Paris! We say to our musician artists: play, play well! but dance at the same time! We say to our great singers: sing, sing well! but for the love of God, dance at the same time! To our professors we say: accompany your discourses with dance! While dancing song or words we begin to live them; we begin to understand what one sings or what one says; we begin to live the verbal or musical emotions.

Come with me to Epirus, help me to found a small ideal country which will be a model for the entire world.(Duncan, 1914:18)

Here dance and the ideal life become synonymous. As their primary goal, people must express their true emotions in all they undertake in their lives. But, Raymond argues, this truly expressive life cannot be lived in Paris, a luxurious city with cars and avenues; it can only be achieved in the mountains of Greece where no avenues mar the landscape and only splendorous nature exists. In 1903 when Raymond and Isadora went to Greece the country was still embroiled in a war with Turkey over the island of Crete. In 1914 Raymond refers to the "troubled situation" in Greece but insists that it remains the only place in which to establish this ideal community where the arts can facilitate a harmonious life (Steichen, 1963: opposite plates 84-87).

Mary Beegle's writing about dance focuses less on the benefits of dancing than the other writers analyzed here. She writes about dance within the context of the theory and practice of pageantry; the pageant itself will help unify and elevate people in their local and national communities. She offers sound practical instructions—precise, concise, and remarkably contemporary. She even discusses everyday issues such as the importance of regular attendance, the need to rehearse on the stage or ground on which the performance will occur, the kind of practice clothing to wear, the reasons for dancing in bare feet, and the like. Into these practical suggestions she weaves revolutionary pedagogical guidelines that encourage dance directors democratically to teach their pageant dancers how to discover their own dance movements and compose their own dances. These instructions differ from traditional hierarchical dance-teaching practices of that time where the dance director created the entire dance sequence and then taught it to the dancers.

Beegle's chapters on natural dancing introduced theoretical principles for and practical guidelines about what came to be called modern dance. The power of her understanding of this form of dance increases when we look at what she claims natural dance is not. She thinks it must not become just a system of rigid rules and carefully planned steps handed down from the past to carry on a tradition; it goes beyond physical training; it is not limited to specialists who labor for years perfecting difficult artificial poses and steps; it is not a superfluous part of drama or opera to show off the skills of dancers and soloists. Beegle's attitudes reflect radical utopian notions especially in her belief that natural rhythmic dance can provide deep personal satisfaction to large numbers of people who need not be professionals. This satisfaction comes from dance which expresses dramatic ideas because historically (in ancient Greek times), Beegle asserts, the first and primary function dance served was pantomimic and was therefore emotionally expressive. The Greeks integrated dance, in those days, into drama, closely linked it with music and song; and it expressed ideas deeply valued by the participants.

For Helen Moller, like Raymond Duncan, Arcadia in ancient Greece serves as the model cultural context in which free and natural dancing must occur: there dancing embodied "natural grace and beauty" (Moller, 1918:25) and allowed free expression, which the current Victorian values did not favor. In ancient Greece the arts were united; in the Greek language one word encompassed dance, music, drama, poetry. When one studies dance history, Moller asserts, one learns about the social history of a people; in their social customs one finds their value system. Thus, turning to the arts of ancient Greece is logical since the first democratic form of government evolved there.

Natural dance, like that of the ancient Greeks, Moller hopes, can develop in America at this time because reforms have begun to change people's values and behavior. She refers to Prohibition in which she placed high hopes. In contrast to Isadora, she believes the increasingly diverse community in America will enhance this opportunity to improve life: "Our 'melting pot' is mingling the most vital blood of every enlightened race under the sun, thus obliterating national traits discovered to be disadvantageous and creating a new people devoid of belittling prejudices, fresh, strong and original in its creative impulses" (Moller, 1918:29). Here in her choice of words "enlightened race" and "obliterating national traits" Moller reflects the hierarchical racial attitudes still common among educated people of this late Victorian period. She identifies the rejection of a dependence on Europe for standards and trends in the arts and ideas as another contributing factor to the current positive cultural context. She explains the new situation this way:

> We are rapidly ridding ourselves of our old world heritage of drunkenness, profligacy and phariseeism. With respect to drink we are becoming

temperate almost to the point of abstention; over-eating is entirely out of fashion; many of our wealthiest families set examples of simple living, discouraging arrogant display, idleness and class distinctions. All our tendencies are toward nobler ideals. Psychologically, we are in a most fortunate position to begin—with our dancing, at least—where the Arcadians left off. (Moller, 1918:33)

Moller's oversimplification of the current American social environment characterizes much of her reasoning throughout the book. In her attempt to convince her readers of the benefits of natural dancing, she exaggerates the positive effects of Prohibition and the other reforms that were implemented in America in the first twenty years of the twentieth century. She depends on the truth and applicability of the "nobler ideals" for all her readers who must have had leisure time to take her classes and extra money to pay for them.

Similar to Isadora Duncan, Margaret H'Doubler claims that the study of dance history reveals basic threads which tie dance together. Depending on philosopher Yrjo Hirn for her interpretation, H'Doubler describes dance history using the developmental theory of history where humanity progresses from childlike and primitive stages to the most advanced adult, civilized scientific society of today. Her concept of dance history reveals her complex view of dance as a physical activity, an educational opportunity, a social force, and an art. The story of art, she asserts, reveals the true history of humankind. She accepts dance as the first art from which the others emerged. Dance became a social force when human beings came together in groups to dance in celebration of their religious and spiritual needs. Basically three types of dances exist: religious dances, dramatic or historic dances for love and war, and dances that imitate animals and nature. As human beings became more civilized, she continues, dance developed into an art at the time of ancient classical Greece. Dance degenerated to mere entertainment during Roman times and re-emerged with artistic potential during the Middle Ages in rural festivities where dancing became free, spontaneous, and symbolic. This type of dance was balanced by the developing professional dance in the courts of the noble and wealthy whose leisurely life style allowed them ample time to practice elaborate, technical, and intricate dances that they performed in the courts. These two streams of dance continued until the 1900s, claims H'Doubler, when people reacted against these artificial and sterile forms by seeking to return to the Greek ideal "founded on laws of natural motion and rhythm" (DPE, 1925:27). The Greeks, H'Doubler reiterates, knew the educational value of dancing. She ends her summary of dance history by noting that dance continues to develop. "In making an historical analysis of the dance we find that the one perfect medium of expression of the inborn sense of rhythm that exists in all people, is the dance" (MD, 1921:8). H'Doubler agrees with Isadora Duncan, Raymond Duncan, and Mary Beegle, that rhythm serves as the binding force in dance history.

Not only does H'Doubler recount the history of dance, but she also identifies its varying functions in different cultural contexts. She recognizes dance as an important part of recreation and amusement. In her own time many people frequent dance halls and enjoy dance in the movies to satisfy their need for self-expression and gain a wider movement experience than they have in their everyday lives. The popular dances of her day, the one step and the fox-trot, H'Doubler claims, do not satisfactorily provide creative outlets for self-expression. H'Doubler uses these examples of popular dance to buttress her arguments for the development of educational dance as creative and self-expressive, associated with the interpretation of great uplifting music.

Margaret Morris places her democratic application of the study of movement, music, and painting into the cultural context of the early twentieth century. People, she argues, spend too much time indoors engaged in activity which leads to muscle weaknesses. They lead stressful lives and do not experience much harmony in their daily work rhythms. Her system can counteract this state of affairs. Historically, all people danced "before the tyranny of the Italian ballet technique dominated the dancing of all civilized peoples" (Morris, 1926:83). Thus, it is logical for everyone to return to their birthright and dance in the manner similar to the earliest democratic people, the Greeks.

The social and historical forces of the past, agree these dancer-writers, have caused dancing to degenerate to a non-art status. The dance of ancient Greece, they claim, offers the model which guides them to reject the existing forms and create a new expressive dance form which speaks for people of the current time and is based on natural movement. In the next chapter I examine what they mean by natural movement.

4

The Body, Movement, and Dance Movement

Dancer-writers of all eras discuss these essential features: the materials or tools of dance are the dancer's body, everyday movement, and dance movement. When dancing, a dancer performs a dance composed of dance movements which are transformed from everyday movements. A more complete examination of topics intrinsic to a theoretical explanation of dance was published in my *Dance-Based Dance Theory*.

This study of the dancer-writers' understanding of the dancer's tools starts with an analysis of Isadora Duncan's views. Isadora's ideas about the body, including advocacy of women's clothing reform, reflect the influence of the American Delsartians who value the beauty and grandeur of a woman's nude body. In America during the 1860s, 1870s, and 1880s followers of Francois Delsarte, a French researcher of human emotions and teacher of natural acting techniques, applied his teachings to elocution, public speaking, and then to health and hygiene. Developers of his training methods evolved exercise systems which early modern dancers integrated into their dance training. Isadora believed the dancer's body, the instrument of the dance, must move unrestricted by any binding clothes. Only the simplest clothing must be used for dancing; if possible the dancer should dance nude (Duncan, 1928:55). Other groups in the physical culture movement besides the Delsartians, advocated the beauty of the nude body, free to be expressive but not seen as erotic or sexual. Unrestricted by clothing, the body, asserts Isadora, moves freely in harmony with nature (Duncan, 1928:54), sensing the space and shape of the stage or other location where the dancing takes place (Duncan, 1928:64). Feet and arms too must be bare, not only to show their beauty but because, unencumbered, they can move freely. This free body radiates a special kind of natural beauty. To gain knowledge of this natural beauty the dancer must live it; then the body becomes a living exponent of beauty. The force of the soul guides the body in gaining knowledge of its inherent beauty. The soul's impulses and inspiration, Isadora declares, must not be deadened by the stern power of the brain (Duncan, 1928:51). With a free spirit the highest intelligence lives in the freest body (Duncan, 1928:61).

These ideas about the body contain the central recurrent theme in Isadora's theory of dance: the soul guides the body's movements in harmony with nature. These words reflect two of the central intellectual influences on her theoretical understanding of dance. The Romantics who want to return to a non-industrialized, bucolic environment proclaim "Harmony with nature" as their slogan. The spiritualists among the utopian idealists preach that the soul's spiritual force, guiding people's instinctive love, will overcome the world's problems. Also evident in Isadora's ideas about the body is her anti-rational view: the spirit must control the "stern power of the brain." Except for this one reference, the mind-body dichotomy, common in discussions of her day, does not recur in Isadora's writings. Instead, she grounds her principles in the unity of body and soul, not only for the dancer's tools but also in composition, performance, and education. Knowledge, she claims, comes from love, instinct, and emotion (Duncan, 1928:99). Her concept of the body centers on its spiritual resources rather than on its anatomical properties or perceptual abilities.

Many of her concepts about dance derive from her rejection of ballet. For hundreds of years the French Academy at the Paris Opera set the standards for ballet. Ballet, as Isadora repeatedly criticizes, restricts the body and its expression. Her rejection of ballet applies to all its constrictions: its aristocratic origins, its subjugation of women, its upper-class support, its artificial subject matter, its restrictive costumes, and its unnatural technique. To prevent ballet's harmful effects on dance from continuing, dancers must challenge the authority of the French Academy. Besides, Isadora proclaims, ballet does not fit the tall and supple bodies of American women (Duncan, 1928:49). These women must dance their own newly created dance, one that speaks for the American soul. American women are too independent to perform predetermined movements, she claims, and they are too active to be deformed by ballet shoes and corsetted costumes (Duncan, 1928:56).

Whereas to compose ballet dances choreographers rearrange predetermined movements found in the traditional vocabulary of "classical" dance, Isadora repeatedly stresses that everyday movement provides the major source of dance movement in her free dance. She explains how these everyday movements communicate: internally motivated human gestures directly express thoughts and feelings of every state of being with great power. And the reverse is true: movement experienced in the external world can give rise to inner responses (Duncan, 1928:103). Isadora recommends studying the movement of children as a source for dance, though nature remains her main source of dance movement (Duncan, 1928:54). Since all things on earth are subject to the pull of gravity, nature generates and controls all movement and manifests the pattern of attraction and repulsion, resistance and yielding (Duncan, 1928:55, 90). One sees this pattern in the motion of ocean waves, of sound, of light, in wind, in the seasons, in the movement of animals, especially of birds in flight (Duncan, 1928: 68). The quality of repose in the bird's swiftest flight (Duncan, 1928:90) exemplifies natural wavelike internal rhythm which natural dance movement should embody. For Isadora, the flowing wave pattern counters the static poses and positions of traditional ballet.

Everyday movements of people and animals, Isadora points out, have much to teach us. Movement of all things in nature corresponds to and depends on the form of that thing. She offers the example of a beetle to illustrate this concept: it moves as it does because of its shape; the beetle's shape dictates its movement (Duncan, 1928:57). Here and in her references to the wave patterns in light and sound, Duncan's ideas reflect the teachings of her friend the famous biologist Ernst H. Haeckel. Dancers, she insists, should study the movements of a wide variety of animals such as fish, birds, reptiles; even "primitive man" in his dances moves his body in harmony with nature (Duncan, 1928:78).

Dance movement for Isadora must be flowing, undulating, and rhythmic. Dancers can find these qualities in the natural movement patterns of everyday life: walking, running, skipping, rolling, stirring, rocking, swinging. Some kinds of movements found in inanimate nature also serve as sources of dance movement. As examples she cites opposing forces of natural rhythmic phenomena which suggest emotional states: the frenzy of a tempest, the passion of a storm, and the gentleness of a breeze (Duncan, 1928:102). These ideas reflect a romantic interpretation of nature where writers attribute human qualities to natural occurrences.

Dance movements, Isadora proclaims, must speak eloquently as the words of a prayer. The dancer's soul guides the conversion of everyday movement into dance movement, to be luminous like moving clouds. To achieve this challenging goal the dancer must find successive movements, that is, each one will have within it the seeds from which will evolve the next movement in natural unending sequences (Duncan, 1928:56). The dancer's "will" develops these movements as they emerge from the highest evolved form of the human body (Duncan, 1928:55). By "will" she means instinct, intuition, internal drive; "highest evolved form" reflects a Darwinian analysis of the human animal. One finds a model for natural unending sequences of movement in the earthy positions of Greek dancing seen on ancient vase painting and *bas* reliefs (Duncan, 1928:58). But today's dancers, warns Isadora, must go beyond ancient Greek movements to discover their own. Though human dance movement should be as rhythmic and flowing as movements found in nature, dance movement, she clarifies, is separate from nature, because it must be original (Duncan, 1928:79). Dancers must discover their own and not imitate others' movements. How Isadora discovers these original movements is discussed with her ideas about composition in Chapter 5.

Isadora's understanding of dance movement reflects the naturalism or organicism popular among the anti-academy artists of the time. The requirement that dance movement originate from the soul in the human body and transmit a spiritual quality also reflects the anti-Victorianism of the American Delsartians who loathed the devalued status and restricted freedom of the human body which still prevailed in much of Europe and America.

Raymond Duncan, like Isadora, also conceives of movement in biological terms. Movement, Raymond claims, is the common denominator of all matter, living and dead, because it is composed of molecules in motion. He gives examples of how motion is central to electricity, wind, water, tree growth, animal action, and even the production of a chair by means of the carpenter's movements. "Thus every phenomenon is only the result, the expression of a movement" (R. Duncan, 1914:4). In his concept of "every phenomenon," he includes the movement of the cells in our minds. In this way he connects the thoughts of Socrates to our lives today since without movements of our minds, the ideas of Socrates would not have been passed on to us. He explains this idea further:

> And I am sure that without our ability for rhythmic motion we could not sense the truths of Socrates in experiencing the beauties toward which he directs us. In the same way all the beauties of all the divine great men are more or less lived by us by reason of our ability to respond or be directed by their movements. (R. Duncan, 1914:6)

For Raymond "rhythmic motion" connects all matter and integrates understanding ourselves with our mental or physical history.

Movement not only unites all phenomenon, declares Raymond, it connects the study of all parts of nature and the universe. Great astronomers, he surmises, understand the motion of the stars because their bodies have experienced motion. Geographers who study the earth, mountains, volcanoes, oceans, and islands sense the motion of these features of the planet in their bodies and transfer that knowledge to their maps. Here Raymond's explanation of bodily sensitivity psychologists later identify as the kinesthetic sense. He offers geologists and orchestra conductors as other examples to illustrate how motion is the binding force for learning and conveying knowledge.

Raymond's ideas about the molecular structure of movement reflect his knowledge of developments in science at that time. Revolutionary scientific discoveries occurred in the late 1800s which changed laypeople's understanding of reality: the speed of light in 1862 (by J. B. L. Foucault), electromagnetism in 1864 (by James Clerk Maxwell), radio waves in 1895 (by Marconi), the electron, and the first atomic particle, in 1897 (by J. J. Thomson). Einstein expounded his theory of relativity in 1904. These new concepts of reality permanently changed the field of philosophy where flow, flux, and change became the common denominator of the all material world. Henri Bergson, an influential philosopher of the day, described this characteristic of reality as duration. These ideas are strikingly similar to Rudolf Laban's major concept of movement (See Maletic and Alter, 1991). Raymond applied this new scientific and philosophical undestanding of reality to his study of gymnastics and dance.

Raymond brings his unified world-view to the features of each individual. When he refers to a human being, he means the entire being: "muscles, feeling, mind, and soul" (R. Duncan, 1914:2). He does not even consider the mind-body dichotomy found in so many discussions of dance by other writers of dance theory after 1930. "Human beings are instruments," he asserts; their main function is to work, not to be amused or improve, or be healthy or even righteous (R. Duncan, 1914:2). With the idea of a well-functioning machine in mind, Raymond claims that a person's body must work well. If it works like a well-oiled machine, he continues, this harmonious experience in itself will lead to happiness; then life becomes worth living. This experience of harmonious work movement, he claims, can transform thoughts and influence other people and the earth itself. These observations reflect those made by French exercise theorists, Etienne Jules Marey, Georges Demeny, and Paul Souriau (1852-1926). Souriau's The Aesthetics of Movement (1889) depends heavily on Marey and Demeny's work (see Chapter 6 below). This action-oriented view of work as inherently satisfying, reflects the stance of the rational recreationists who preached against time spent frivolously in useless degenerating activity.

Mary Beegle's chapters on dance contrast with those of Raymond and Isadora Duncan. She does not consider the details of the body and its faculties. The body which displays this rhythmic movement, Beegle claims, is "used as a medium of expression for the mind" (Beegle and Crawford, 1916:193). Beegle defends dancing as a rational endeavor; the mind governs the emotional expression which the body exhibits through dance. Since she focuses on making dances, she only comments in passing on the body-senses-mind unity which creating art work requires. Because Beegle and Crawford's book served as a text, the rational component of art-making provides a logical argument to make in academic contexts. This rational emphasis contrasts with Isadora Duncan's stress on the soul's expression and with Raymond's focus on the smooth working of a unified body.

Like most of the other dancer-writers, Helen Moller uses the metaphor, "instrument," to describe the body. Moller identifies the sentient body as a remarkable instrument. It houses the soul and mind and enables people to enjoy "enlivening and actuating" movements and expressions (Moller, 1918:81). These expressive movements can be either thoughts or emotions. Reflecting Delsartian influence, Moller pays special attention to the facial expressions of her dancers and points these out in the captions of the photographs in her book: "The speaking eye, the mirror-like, plastic countenance and gracefully responsive limbs form an instrument of interpretation capable of imaging forth the subtlest shade of meaning" (Moller, 1918:34). Though she uses the terms "mind" and "body" separately, she stresses the unity of all human capabilities: senses, thoughts, and emotions.

Moller, like Isadora Duncan, ardently espouses clothing reform. The second of her six chapters centers entirely on "The Tyranny of Clothes." She speaks adamantly against "fashion" and even blames the decadent state of dancing and sculpture on it. The corset and the pointed toe high-heeled shoe of high-fashion, Moller believes, must be eliminated. The human body, in her view, needs to move freely with no impediments. Her praise of the elasticity and strength of the feet, shows anatomical awareness: "Their structure is necessarily complex—a finely organized, shapely, mass of jointed bones, powerful muscles, ligaments, tendons, and sensitive nerves, with a circulatory system which depends for its efficiency upon freedom of movement of every part" (Moller, 1918:49). She values freedom for the feet as well as for movement of the entire body.

Moller even considers the skin in her explanation of the unhygienic limitation of clothes. She quotes a well-known authority, Lieutenant Mueller of the Danish Army, to back up her ideas about uncovered skin. Exercising without clothes, he insists, is best for the body; it allows the skin to breathe and expell poisonous gas, especially carbolic acid. Health reformers during this time popularized this idea. Some physicians in Europe and America became rich and famous by encouraging nudity or prescribing special clothing, such as that made from all wool, to enable their patients' skin to breathe. Moller agrees with Isadora Duncan; the freely clad or nude body allows the greatest freedom to express any true thought or emotion while dancing.

Fundamental principles, Moller claims, guide body movement. One of these principles is opening and closing or folding and unfolding. The two ways she explains this principle exemplify the dual focus she maintains in her discussion of the body. "Opening and closing" refers to natural emotional expression, whereas "folding and unfolding" stems from an anatomical analysis of body movement. Several of the photographs show dancers' arms or legs moving in opposite directions: up and down, back and forward; and with contrasting feelings: lyrical and mischievous, shy and free, humble and proud. Her exercises build on the Delsartian principle of opposites.

Dance movement, Moller insists, must be based on Greek sculpture. She trusts an expert on Greek sculpture, John Warrack, who believed the movements found in Greek sculpture represent natural dance movement and are not based on art conventions. The primary emotions portrayed in Greek sculpture, Warrack claimed, were repose and serenity. To these emotions Moller adds joy. Moller's natural dancing focussed on expressing these emotions because they were predominant in Greek sculpture. Since dance movement must be original and spontaneous, never hackneyed, Moller requires her dancers to interpret the Greek positions.

As most of our other writers do, Margaret H'Doubler also calls the body the dancer's instrument but points out that all other artists share this instrument: painters, musicians, actors, and writers. The body, as the dancer's instrument, H'Doubler reiterates, works independently of any external agency unlike other arts which use external tools and inorganic materials, such as musical instruments, paints, and paper. The body, she claims, is the sensitive dance-art instrument, because "all mental activity (both thought and feeling) tends to express itself in muscular and glandular activity" (DPE, 1925:15). Here H'Doubler reflects knowledge of early twentieth-century experimental psychology which views the mind and body as an interactive unit. H'Doubler agrees with Isadora Duncan and Beegle about the role of rhythm. It serves as the central regulator of the body's functions and, thus, guides all art and dance. She cites turn-of-the-century aesthetician Yrjo Hirn as her source for her ideas on the central role of rhythm in art. The basic function of rhythm was widely accepted by experts in many other disciplines during this period, including John Dewey, her teacher at Columbia Teachers College, who develops Bergson's ideas from a few years before. The habits of the inexperienced body, H'Doubler insists, must be guided and controlled to prevent them from hampering or limiting self-expression. The body "must be more sensitive and responsive than even the most finely tuned instrument if it is to respond instantaneously to every flicker of emotion in the dancer's mind, from the lightest mirth to despair" (DPE, 1925:57). H'Doubler uses the body-mind dichotomy in her writing, but she values creative self-expression more than the control of the mind over the unschooled body .

Unlike our other authors, H'Doubler incorporates the kinesthetic sense in her discussion of the body's sensitivity, and utilizes Raymond Duncan's ideas about the body's inherent knowledge to describe its applications. In both of her books H'Doubler explains how the kinesthetic sense plays a pivotal role in schooling the body. Dancing develops this sense because it provides an outlet for impressions gathered by the other senses, and these sensory impressions require expression. The creative imagination, she points out, enables students to express their unique experiences in a vital and unifying manner while dancing: "When thought, feeling and action are coordinated, free and sponta-neous movements" facilitate the expression of the imagination (MD, 1921:9). Reflecting the influence of Freud's ideas of repression and sublimation, reason, she warns, must not too rigidly control our feelings; they must have a creative outlet.

Before the creative work of dance-making can commence, H'Doubler explains, students need to control random everyday movement which occurs reflexively to express feelings. This random yet expressive movement is not yet dance; it provides the seeds for dancing. Although all movement, she asserts, is essentially constructed from the pattern of expansion and contraction, move-ment must be "subjected to the harmonizing influence of rhythm, or time sequence," and then "dance proper comes into being" (DPE, 1925:15). Rhythm not only organizes the body's functions, but, for H'Doubler, it controls art, music, and time in the everyday world. She defines rhythm as: "action and rest—control and release; it is measured motion—a periodic repetition" (DPE, 1925:15). (H'Doubler's definition is not quite accurate; rhythm is a repeated uneven pattern like a heartbeat and not merely a set of repeated beats like a clock ticking which her definition implies.) Rhythm gives movement ease and grace, and, therefore, enables dancers to convert everyday movement into dance movement.

As do our other dancer-writers, Eleanor Elder thinks of the body and its powers as a unity of physical, mental, and emotional experience, not just bone, flesh, and muscle. To educate this unified body in the ideal manner, she suggests three goals: "Healthy development, Control and Expression" (Elder, 1918:2). For men and boys, wrestling satisfies the need for "healthy development," while for women and girls, dancing will. The public does not consider wrestling, a body-contact and combative activity, appropriate for women. In dancing women and girls gain "control" by experiencing balance in a relaxed, alert, and confident manner, the way a baby experiences balancing when taking his or her first steps alone. Elder offers this example as the only one to explain what she means by control and "balance." Drama, she believes, best teaches "expression," and dance is closely linked to Drama, whence its value in achieving this goal. This physical training for expression, she insists, frees students from their self-consciousness and she hopes this experience in freedom of expression will last a lifetime. Though brief, Elder's discussion of the materials of dance integrates the body and the senses and then offers examples of everyday movements which best suit training in dancing.

Like the other writers, Margaret Morris discusses the body but connects it to dance technique and composition, the central foci of her writing. In 1926, she acknowledges, many people engage in a wide variety of physical activities: walking, running, games, sports, gymnastics, boxing, and physical training in schools. People participate in these activities, she observes, without having their minds stimulated along with their bodies. In contrast to these other activities, her system of exercise unites the mind with the body by utilizing each person's creative capability. In her description of the most suitable clothing to wear for dancing, she concentrates on the teacher's need to really see the body. She designed a tunic which allows the teacher to observe the student's posture and still allow for modesty: a cotton bathing suit with a short skirt sewed on below the waist. In total agreement with our other authors, Morris insists on bare feet to allow them to become strong and agile and also to let teacher view their positions. Lastly, "I need hardly say that corsets are not worn" (Morris, 1926: 33). Like Moller, Morris believes strong muscles can provide ample support for the internal organs, making corsets unnecessary. Her exercises can correct the bad posture caused by muscle weakness. The Greek positions she adapted from Raymond Duncan, she points out, help alleviate this problem.

The human being is richly endowed with a sensory system, which Morris believes must be stimulated in children from a very young age. Morris developed her educational program deliberately to educate each sense: music and sound for the ears; singing, discussing, and acting for the voice; painting, design, and drawing for the eyes; movement and creative dance for the muscles. Natural training of all the senses, Morris claims, gives the mind flexibility and increases perception and concentration and constructively connects the mind and body.

Movement for Morris must be "natural:" it must be done "without contortion, strain, or over-development" (Morris, 1926:19) regardless of one's surroundings and circumstances. The other movement activities in which people engage, such as walking, running, and boxing, have become unnaturally competitive and no longer directly connect people to their lives and work. For Morris, people must practice movements which harmonize with their daily experience and contribute to their sense of well-being. She sets out to accomplish this with her Margaret Morris Movement (MMM) techniques.

Morris bases her dance movements on the positions found on Greek vase paintings and on the natural movements people can do, such as walk, run, jump, and hop. She experimented with these movements and found ways of exaggerating the body's positions in these basic activities. Many of the photographs in her book picture her and her students in an accentuated large step with the upper body tipped quite far back and one bent leg raised high forward. This position seems to be her trademark because it appears in many of the pictures in her later books as well. No dance movement, she believes, is ugly or stupid if it is natural and can be done without strain. Her discussion of the body, the senses, movement, and dance movement turns on physical properties and experience. She uses few metaphors, and unlike many of the other writers I analyze, she does not identify the body as an instrument.

The body moving naturally is the major theme of these writers in their discussions of the body, movement, and dance movement. All but Morris label the body as the dancer's instrument. Though most do not discuss the senses, Morris emphasizes all the senses, while H'Doubler focuses on the kinesthetic, reflecting her scientific approach. They all agree on an integrated concept of the body which includes the mind and senses, and they agree that the body must be free to move. This means that the dancer dances with no corset, is barefoot, and wears loose flowing clothing which leaves arms, legs, or both uncovered. Natural movement found in pictures of people dancing on Greek vase paintings serves as the model. To those positions our authors add walking, running, hopping, skipping, jumping, and so forth. Natural everyday movements become dance movements when they fit the body harmoniously. "Harmonious" or "in harmony with nature" implies non-competitive, non ballet-like movement which does not display virtuosity. All of these dancer-writers evolved methods to teach their students how to use natural movement in choreographing their dances, the subject of the next chapter.

5
Natural Dance Composition, its Performance, and its Relation to the Other Arts

For our dancer-writers the activity of dancing centers on composing and performing original dances; each discusses different aspects of the process. Though they recognize dancing as a performing art, most concentrate on the creative part of the process, the composing and dancing, while de-emphasizing the final process and product in performance.

Isadora Duncan treats dance composition thoroughly. Her discussion encompasses types of choreographers, types of dances, sources of choreography, as well as her method of making dances. Composing a dance, she informs her readers, requires a lot of work (Duncan, 1928:103). Isadora believes three types of choreographers exist: the first uses prearranged movements from gymnastic systems. The second uses the mind to lead into movement which comes out of remembered feelings and experiences. The third, inspired by the soul, converts natural movements of the body into luminous fluidity moving to inwardly heard music (Duncan, 1928:51). This third is Isadora's model. Truly creative dancers (choreographers) discover natural movement; they do not invent steps or imitate others' movements (Duncan, 1928:102). "Invent" implies that the mind directs the body; mind-directed dance movement would be too "rational" and not natural. Creative dancers, Isadora believes, compose dances with universal appeal although they generate dance movement from within their own spiritual experience.

Isadora derives her dance compositions from a variety of sources: spiritual, mystical, or natural. These categories often blend but in some of her explanations Isadora emphasizes one more the other. When she claims that dances come from the soul, or the solar plexus, which is the temporal home of the soul, she stresses the spiritual source of dance. When she claims that art emerges from the external world of everyday occurrences and that dances must reveal the unrefined beauty of these occurrences, nature provides the source. When she asserts that our human bodies are part of nature and that we must discover movements which express the soul of these natural forms, she combines the spiritual and the natural (Duncan, 1928:102).

The human body, claims Isadora, as the root of all art created by human beings is also central to dance. Isadora reminds her readers how artists, painters, and sculptors of all ages have valued the human body as an object of divine beauty. In this tradition, therefore, dancers should choose movements which express the strength, health, nobility, ease, and serenity of living things. In this context Isadora repeats her assertion that a universal unity exists between form and movement (Duncan, 1928:102). In her writing she does not suggest negative events and circumstances, such as war, poverty, or political oppression as appropriate subjects for dances, even though she danced about these subjects in some of her most famous dances. In instances such as this, her selective and idealized writing does not always represent the reality of her work or her total vision.

How does one choreograph a dance? Isadora gives two hints: Seeking the center of motor power, she stands still for hours with her hands folded over her solar plexus (the place above the navel and below the base of the sternum). She waits in this position, she reports, to find a basic movement from which another will emerge. This movement must exteriorize the fullness of her feeling; the impulse must then spread to the next expressive movement (Duncan, 1928:99). She balances this description with instructions about what not to do. Do not just rearrange a series of steps or make an arbitrary set of mechanical combinations. Her second hint concentrates on how to craft this expressive and basic first movement. The ground plan should be a wave because all energy—light, sound, and gravity—expresses itself through a wave. The dancer, she asserts, looks for the secret of the perfect proportion of line and curve in this waving movement (Duncan, 1928:68). Duncan highlights dance as a creative and vital art to help audiences recognize dance as more than popular entertainment.

When Duncan speaks of the dancer she means choreographer. For her these two roles are indistinguishable. A truly creative dancer, she insists, does not imitate others' movements but chooses ones which the individual generates to express something greater than the self (Duncan, 1928:52). This dancer will dance the freedom of women (Duncan, 1928:63) and will belong to humanity not just to a single nation (Duncan, 1928:62). Here the women's suffrage movement and the utopian vision of an international community guide Isadora's definition of "dancer."

Isadora discusses the aesthetic intent of her dances by comparing them to other kinds of dance. Just as she differentiates among kinds of choreographers, she categorizes dances into profane dances, which aim their message at the senses, and sacred dances, which the spirit receives (Duncan, 1928:50). She intends her dances to reach the spirits of her spectators. The themes of her dances convey either spiritual, democratic, natural, or feminist messages: they express the moral, the healthful, or the beautiful. She believes her spiritual dances convey the most noble expression of human life and reflect the call of the divine. These dances must contribute harmony, joy, strength, and courage to people's lives and must "glow" and "pulse" to reach the pinnacle of the human spirit. Her dances must show the fortitude, justice, and kindness of our heroes, the purity of women, and the inspiring and tender love of our mothers (Duncan, 1928:98). In her dances she does not represent an individual woman, she claims, but she symbolizes humanity (Duncan, 1928:85). Not only must her dances move people spiritually, but in them she seeks to connect the audience to nature. While in her solos she conveys plastic (mobile) movements like those of the Greek chorus, her dances also translate the power of gravitation in the universe by expressing the serenity and inner rhythm of emotion (Duncan, 1928:99).

While performing, Isadora explains, each dancer must remain an individual. No two dancers, she insists, must look or dance alike (Duncan, 1928:58). Here again she rejects ballet training since it requires each dancer to learn and execute exactly the same movements. Ballet companies choose dancers of similar height and weight, and when performing in the corps de ballet, these dancers strive to move in complete unison. She rebels against the star system of ballet when she defines dancing as an egoless state. In true dance, she claims, individuals forget their bodies and express only the thoughts and feelings of their souls.

In addition to her discussion of the aesthetic intent of her dances, Isadora describes what she hopes the audience will receive aesthetically. She wants the audience to participate actively and not just sit passively being entertained (Duncan, 1928:123). Because dancers express the movements of nature, she trusts the audience members will intuitively recognize the natural source and spiritual message of her dances. She believes the audience will feel the movement of light intermingled with the thought of whiteness and will respond to the dance as a prayer. These ideas embody the utopian romantic concept of art as divinely inspired and intuitively understandable by the masses. Performances, Isadora asserts, should be offered free of charge so audiences of all classes can participate in her invocation (Duncan, 1928:143). When possible in Russia, audiences attended her concerts at no charge; at times, such as these free concerts, she put her radical economic views into practice.

In contrast to Isadora, Raymond Duncan does not discuss dance composition in detail. A dance like all the other arts, he insists, is based on the angular movement he found in his study of Greek movement. Reflecting a Delsartian standard of balance, Raymond defines a harmonious dance as "a truly artistic symmetrical expression" (R. Duncan, 1914:15). He then ties his concept of a harmonious dance to its performance. When dancing these kinds of dances, dancers should absorb the harmonious movements of the universe as should audience members when seeing them. Audiences watching this kind of dance, Raymond predicts in agreement with Isadora, will be stimulated and will therefore begin to study dance. In his consideration of dance performances, Raymond unites the performers with the audience members as he connects teachers with students (see Chapter 7 below).

Dance, for Raymond, holds a special place in the universal scheme of events. Like his view of the universe, he holds a unified concept of the arts. Music and song vocally express the "movements of dance and gymnastics" (R. Duncan, 1914:5). Dance and the repetition of its rhythmic formations, he continues, contribute to the development of beautiful character in people. Since dance and gymnastic consist of pure movement, Raymond claims, they represent the resurrection of "preceding life concentrated in a symmetrical melody" (R. Duncan, 1914:6). Thus, gymnastics and dance carry within their experience the history of the human race. Movement, he asserts, connects all events through time. Raymond Duncan's concept of movement's connection with time through history is a linear version of Rudolf Laban's notion that human dance movement represents a sympathetic response to the patterned movements of the molecular pathways of particles in atoms of all matter in the universe.

In contrast to Raymond Duncan, Mary Beegle offers detailed information about dance composition but agrees with him about the role and response of the audience. While giving practical instructions for the function of dance and the training of dancers in a pageant, Beegle's two-part chapter on dance also informs laypeople about basic theoretical principles of composing and performing natural dancing. According to Beegle, none of the current forms of dance— professional dance which requires years of specialized training, the dance used in the schools for physical exercise, or folk dances used for recreation—are appropriate for the dance needs of a pageant. Beegle advocates dramatic and creative dance art: "The purpose of the dance is to achieve creative self-expression through the interpretation of ideas by means of rhythmic movement" (Beegle and Crawford, 1916:193). Natural dancing also gives people an opportunity for expressing meaningful ideas in rhythmic graceful movement. Further, spectators directly experience this expressive dance, since, like music, dance "is emotional . . . and its interpretive value consists in its power to convey emotions to the minds of the audience" (Beegle and Crawford, 1916:197).

Creative, natural self-expression, insists Beegle, reaches all participants of the pageant, players and audience alike.

Natural dancing for Beegle goes beyond living techniques and creative self-expression. Rhythm, Beegle claims, not only binds the entire production together, it also functions in the way dance contributes to the entire drama. Rhythm underpins the process of composing the three types of dance most useful in drama: the plot dance, the illustrative dance, and the dance interlude. Each dance conveys its emotional content by establishing and maintaining the particular rhythm unique to its mood. The four underlying principles— rhythmic progression, mood, action, and climax—guide the composition of each dance.

> Rhythmic progression is the harmonious flow of the action of the dance through the climax to the conclusion. The mood determines the tempo and hence the kind of rhythm, and the whole dance is governed by the action to be expressed. Rhythmic progression, in the practical building of the dance, is the division and the progression of the action worked out through the dramatic laws of repetition, contrast, pause (suspense), and the rise and fall of movement. (Beegle and Crawford, 1916:208)

The mood, Beegle insists, conveys the emotional atmosphere of the scene and determines the tempo of the movement. Action in this context means the structured sequence of movements which interpret the story or plot. Rhythm physically ties the dramatic component parts and the totality of a dance together.

Selecting the mood and its rhythm, for Beegle, initiates the choreographic process. She advises how to proceed from that point. After identifying the proper mood, the choreographer must choose and arrange the steps for the dance. The director, Beegle recommends, should invite the dancers to discover and arrange steps that convey to them the mood and emotional content needed for each scene or interlude in which they will dance.

Beegle explains how to prepare the dancers for their creative responsibility in devising the pageant. Before beginning the physical part of the rehearsal, and the choreographic process itself, Beegle instructs the dance director to present to the dancers the detailed story or plot of the dance which they will perform. Knowledge of the story or mood enables the dancers to understand exactly what emotions and actions their personally-discovered movements should convey. In agreement with Raymond and Isadora Duncan, Beegle repeats, "No dance should ever be taught as a mere combination of steps to be learned by rote"

(Beegle and Crawford, 1916:221).

Beegle not only explains how to compose a dance, she gives instructions about improvising—finding original movement. The clear guidelines Beegle presents for improvising show the depth of her experience and knowledge in teaching creative dance. After the warm-up, dancers practice walking, running, leaping, and twirling in the mood of their dance. Then they practice skipping, a more rhythmically complex locomotor movement, in the mood of the performance and also experiment with a wide variety of other feelings not found in the pageant. In this context she reminds her readers that not all the ways of skipping need to be graceful. Dancers must understand that the object of each exercise "is to express a complete idea in each movement" (Beegle and Crawford, 1916:223). The more the dancers participate in discovering truly expressive movements, Beegle claims, the more absorbed they will be in their rehearsals and the more convinced the audience will be of the meaningfulness of their dancing. This training process, she cautions, proceeds gradually. Beegle urges the director to experiment with group-discovered movement ideas until the dancers satisfactorily construct and completely synchronize it with the music. The music, she insists, must be composed to accompany a specific dance and no other.

Though Beegle and Crawford offer guidelines for indoor pageants, they prefer outdoor settings for their performances. Helen Moller agrees with Beegle: the ideal place for dancing is outdoors, in fields, woods, gardens, or on the seashore. Since this type of dancing, claims Moller, rejuvenates care-laden spirits, nature provides the only setting for this expressive activity to take place. Within this setting, dancers can express their emotions in a true, honest, spontaneous, and free manner. While Moller only uses "divine" or "divinity" a few times in her book, her message, like Raymond Duncan's, reflects this "higher" set of values: natural outdoor settings are best for dancing, the dancing of the ancient Greeks (found in Greek art) again provides the model to follow, and if one dances regularly in the great outdoors, one's health and well-being are virtually insured into old age.

Dancing for Moller means improvising to music, using the positions of people in Greek sculpture. She explains how she enables her students to dance in a Greek manner. They mentally visualize themselves in Arcadia during the Golden Age of Greece. By wearing Greek tunics, studying Greek art and responding to the music she provides for them, her students express themselves freely: "Serene contemplation of a charming landscape, of white clouds floating under a turquoise sky, of flowers, of trees, of shady groves besides rippling streams, the same as with the Arcadians, will obliterate consciousness of self and liberate the real understanding and creative ego" (Moller, 1918:79). This statement characterizes the ideal picture of nature in which members of the back-to-nature movement believed: its feeling of peace and tranquility, its power to stimulate creativity, and its promise to rejuvenate burdened souls.

In agreement with Raymond Duncan, Moller hopes that when audience members watch the dancing of her students, the emotionally truthful and aesthetically satisfying dance will amaze them. They will recognize the artificiality of the other dance forms they see on theater stages of the day with their prearranged steps. The spectators will not sit passively watching but also will want to participate and enjoy the dancers' upright posture, their freedom of physical and emotional expression, and the resulting health.

People require a definite ideal, Moller believes, to satisfy their aesthetic sense. The aesthetic goal she wants to achieve emerges from her broad goal of restoring and developing classic Greek dance by attempting emotionally to re-inhabit Arcady. She offers veiled criticism of some of her contemporaries in the dance field who say their dance also reconstructs ancient Greek or Egyptian dance. Moller describes their dance as "unanimated" (Moller, 1918:61) and creates passive or tense responses in audience members, the kind of tension she has seen in people who watch sports events. Such tension would counteract the emotional goal of experiencing serenity and repose.

Moller identifies several ways to carry out her theoretical aesthetic goal in practice. Dancing outside allows dancers to realize the greatest personal freedom and independence from the earth's support. The students' inherent response to music enhances this freedom; combining music and dance, Moller asserts, brings true happiness (Moller, 1918:101). Participation in natural dancing then enables the dancers to forget their cares and worries: "You are a creature whose birthright is pure joy. Ordinary mortals walk; *you* dance" (Moller, 1918:113). Even when her dancers wear free flowing garments with bare arms and feet, their dancing should have neither sensual nor sexual appeal. The draperies only enable their skin to breathe and allow them to care for their bodies in the most advanced hygienic manner. Thus, the components of natural dancing—an outdoor setting, free flowing draperies, imagined Arcadian peace, stimulating music, the positions of Greek sculpture, or the stories of Greek gods and goddesses—allow the dancers to reach the height of their aesthetic sensibilities.

In today's theater dance, choreographers choose to convey to audiences their personal aesthetic values. Moller's natural dancing differs from this practice in two crucial ways. First, the dancers serve as the primary audience for their dancing; they dance for their own pleasure and well-being. When they dance for others, the result should be to stimulate the audience members to want to dance. The second difference from today's modern dance practice lies in the source of the dancer's aesthetic choices. They are individually generated, not circumscribed by the costume, music, and Greek model for physical position, emotional expression, or story to be interpreted as were Moller's.

Although H'Doubler writes about self-expressive and creative dance experience in her early books, she only discusses composition in brief and general terms. She makes clear what dancing is not: "it is not a combination of erratic movements and gestures distributed at random" (MD, 1921:9). It is not imitation of others' movements, steps, or dances. When composing a dance students must forget the technicalities and "focus attention upon the spirit and structure of the dance" (MD, 1921:9). The study of craft, common to all the arts, explains H'Doubler, enables students to master the structure of the dance while still embodying the spirit in the art. Quoting Havelock Ellis, she defines a dance as controlled form which involves choices about balance, accent, and shading. Nothing extraneous appears in a finished dance. The work of composing a dance uses "conscious thought and effort" (DPE, 1925:185); it is an intellectual activity. In making art, H'Doubler argues, one goes beyond the intellectual to include the spiritual capability. Her ideas about the serious and complex nature of dance composition here stress the rational part of the creative process. The purpose for which she wrote her books explains this focus: to convince academicians who knew nothing about creating art or dancing that the activity of dancing and the study of dance was a worthwhile academic undertaking. Two years after writing *Dance and Its Place in Education*, her efforts met with success since she established a dance major in the Department of Physical Education in the School of Education at the University of Wisconsin.

H'Doubler centers her theory on creative expression, while performance plays a much less important part. She sees the public demand for entertainment as harassment because uninformed audience members do not understand the value of the students' experiential creative process in educational dance. The students should give a performance, she suggests, only if they "spontaneously wish to share the joy which they have found in the dance" (DPE, 1925:209). The experience can be educational if undertaken in that spirit. Echoing Isadora Duncan, H'Doubler claims that in performance the dance completes its artistic function when an audience appreciates it: "for the appreciator it is creation by evocation" (DPE, 1925:13). Like Isadora Duncan, Mary Beegle, and Helen

Moller, H'Doubler prefers that the audience members not watch passively but take an active part in the event. Reflecting her background in pageantry, H'Doubler asserts that a dance-drama is the best type of performance to give because unschooled audience members understand the dramatic content most easily. To maintain the democratic approach to the production, H'Doubler suggests that the dance director list all the dancers' names alphabetically at the end of the program. Her emphasis remains on the creative goal of interpretive dancing.

Compared to the other dancer-writers examined here, Margaret Morris presents the most complete and detailed steps to explain how students progress in their study of composition. To clarify why her system is superior to the other programs of physical culture Morris uses the word "creative." She calls for creative activity in all her students; they begin composing dances when they begin to study her technique system. Everyone, she believes, has the capacity and the desire to create. Artistic activity, she asserts, has a compelling quality because it is done for no other reason than for its own value and counteracts the everyday dullness and ugliness which surround people.

Morris outlines the steps of her composition program. Early in their training, students compose small studies by themselves and in small groups. Group composition helps them learn to cooperate and gain a team experience. They improvise to music, or rhythms of verse, or sounds of percussion instruments. At first they make abstract designs, then as they gain experience, they express ideas or emotions. Morris does not believe in giving students free rein, but she guides them in forming their dances by using principles which apply to all the arts. She agrees with the other dancer-writers about composing dances: creating a dance is not just stringing steps together. In contrast to Duncan and H'Doubler, Morris does not believe dancing is interpreting the feeling music stimulates in the listener. The dance composition must convey the dancer's feeling to the audience, and this occurs when the dancer understands the principles of form and color.

When discussing dance performance, Morris also considers the audience. When she explains the value of arts experience in people's lives, she describes the emotional "uplift" people gain from simply attending an artistic event. This emotional experience produces a natural appeal and motivates them to partici-pate actively in the art. Her theatrical approach to a dance production shows Morris's sensitivity to the audience point of view. She identifies the visual sense as the primary one by which members of a dance audience appreciate the performance. For this reason she wants her students to be aware of the visual design of their dances.

All the dancer-writers agree that dancers must find their own movement when they compose a dance and that the impact of their natural dancing on the audience members will be to stimulate them to want to dance. The emphasis on the aesthetic qualities of a composition vary among our authors. Isadora Duncan claims a dance must express universal spiritual responses to nature. Raymond Duncan requires spiritual expression in symmetrical angular movement derived from his Greek positions. The mood and spirit of the pageant's content, Beegle insists, guides the development of each original dance, while interpreting music ranks as the chief goal in composing a dance for Moller and H'Doubler. The creative experience of composing these dances all agree, takes priority over the dance itself.

Other Arts

Though our authors focus on composing dances, they discuss dance composition in relation to the other arts. They discuss music, especially its rhythmic basis, most frequently. They mostly agree on its central supporting role in dancing.

Music, especially great music, should accompany the free dance Isadora Duncan espouses. She composes her dances to music by composers such as Beethoven, Schubert, Mozart, Chopin, Gluck, and Bach. She urges her students to compose their dances to great classical music because the works of these composers contain universal rhythms. These composers do not invent such rhythms, she claims, but they emerge from the natural underlying principles of life. Debussy's music, she criticizes, emanates from and stimulates the senses; because it lacks spirituality it is inappropriate for dance composition (Duncan, 1928:107). When dancers or choreographers listen to great music, she asserts, they must listen with their souls. Their bodies will react naturally to this music; their heads will lift, their arms will rise, and they will walk toward the light, because music "is the divine wellspring of art" (Duncan, 1928:87). Here Isadora agrees with other artists and philosophers of her day. Music with its non-literal expressivity provides the model toward which the other arts must strive.

The proper costume for dance, Isdora asserts, allows the body to move freely; the feet must be bare to feel the ground. Isadora preferred a Greek tunic and performed in one most of the time. In her schools she also dressed the children in these loose-fitting garments. Reflecting her intense devotion to things Greek, Isadora's ideal costume sharply contrasts with the typical ballet tutu and other elaborate and ornate dance costumes worn by entertainment dancers of the time.

Isadora's comments about music and costume frequently focus on their inherent unity. Charles Fourier, the father of utopian anarchism, popularized the idea about the basic unity of the arts; artists and thinkers including many Symbolist artists, writers, and poets, agreed with this unifying concept. Isadora did also; she agrees with the composer Scriabin when she reiterates how much she wants to see music, art, and dance come together as in ancient Greece (Duncan, 1928:123). She believes dance serves as the bridge between music and poetry (Duncan, 1928:84), though she actually critiques pantomime because it tries to imitate language. The arts communicate in their own language and need not imitate the spoken one (Duncan, 1928:95).

In agreement with Isadora Duncan, music for Helen Moller is a twin of the dance "sharing on equal terms creation and interpretation" (Moller, 1918:69). Rhythm and form unify the primary features of music, dance, and poetry. She counts on music to stimulate her dancers' imaginations:

> Its influence upon physical expression of the unimpeded operation of the subconsciousness will produce instinctive postures, gestures and naturally graceful movements which not only clearly and adequately express the mood and embody the mental image but more than equal the effects of the highest art based upon a mechanical technique. (Moller, 1918:77)

In this passage she praises the power of music to stimulate instinctive, internally generated movements and to create dancing which exceeds the artistic level of ballet, the most well-known competitor of the new "natural" dancing. Moller's use of "subconsciousness" along with "ego" in other statements, indicates her familiarity with the newly popular language of Freudian psychoanalysis. Like Isadora Duncan, she gave dance concerts such as the one in the program (cited in Chapter 2 above) which announced that her ensemble would perform "interpretative" dancing.

Managing the draperies the dancers wear, Moller insists, becomes part of the technique of training, improvising, and performing. Although most Greek sculpture shows the human body without clothes, drapery appears on some figures. The photographs in Moller's book picture children or young women in transparent Greek-style tunics. Most tunics reach below the knee, some above, while some have long trains of fabric to carry, swing, wave, and hide behind. The dancers wear no underwear beneath these tunics which have no sleeves, and are made of only one layer of material. The tunics tie around the waist or higher around the ribs to give a bodice effect. Moller's dedication to exact replication of Greek costumes carries out her goal of transporting her dancers back to Arcady.

Because Margaret H'Doubler wrote in an academic context, she connected dance to more established academic disciplines, especially music, to increase its stature in the eyes of her non-arts colleagues. The study of musical performance and composition in academic institutions had achieved recognition and served as a model for establishing dance as a subject worthy of a university degree. She could easily relate dance to music because of its centrality in her early views about dance composition. In her books written in 1921 and 1925, she bases dance composition on music (see Alter, 1984). Music has always had an organic relationship to dance, she claims, and thus the pairing of the two arts is logical. Music, for H'Doubler, controls dance movements, creates a mood, offers a situation, and stimulates the themes about which students compose dances. Reflecting the influence of Jaques-Dalcroze, H'Doubler explains the value and impact of music: "Its rhythms and harmonies satisfy one of the most fundamental needs of every normal human being, the need for satisfaction of the sense of rhythm that is grounded deep in his physical constitution" (DPE, 1925:148). Like the Duncans and Mary Beegle, H'Doubler also views rhythm as the main influential factor in all the arts. Beyond its rhythmic structure music speaks to our feelings. "The dancer by responding to the stimulus of the music can translate its sounds back into the emotions which inspired them" (DPE, 1925:148). In her curriculum, students must study the structure of music: its rhythmic basis, its laws of harmony, its tempi, variations, and history. This immersion in music, H'Doubler declares, will contribute to students' emotional responses when they prepare to compose their dances.

In addition to music, H'Doubler briefly refers to the other arts when she discusses composition. She has a unified view of the arts; similar principles of art and craft guide them all: the experience of beauty, rhythm, variety within limits, proportion, balance or symmetry, unity, and harmony of the whole (DPE, 1925:227). The arts express emotional experience that cannot be externalized in any other way: "Art remains ever the expression of the world's soul" (DPE, 1925:11).

H'Doubler offers precautionary comments about the other arts. She recommends that dance students use costume and lighting together with music only to enhance the dance. A Greek tunic, her recommended dance costume, and bare feet, she warns, do not alone make for educational dance. She refers to the great popularity of Greek-style dance where dancers did not adhere to rigorous creative goals. By the early 1920s dancers, claiming to be "authentic," in vaudeville and other popular entertainment venues donned Greek tunics and tripped lightly around the stage in time to sweet tinkly music. When students begin to compose dances for dance-dramas (pageants), H'Doubler warns that their dramatic instinct becomes stronger than their dance instinct; thus, the teacher must help convert their dramatic impulses into a more rhythmic and symbolic form. She cautions against the literal quality of pantomimic movement; use it in a dance only if "it is compatible with [the dance's] medium of line and rhythm" (DPE, 1925:217).

Like H'Doubler, Morris views the arts as unified, but she goes beyond the emphasis on music. To enable her students to compose dances well, Morris has them study other arts: drawing, painting and design, and then music. They experience the plastic arts first hand by modelling, carving, pasting, and constructing with cardboard and wood. Even while dancing, Morris's students observe the shapes which each individual and the group makes; they draw the ground plans of their dances. Essential art training, Morris argues, does not require students to imitate the great masters, the current practice in art study. Instead her students experience the common features shared by all arts in their composition: line, form, space, texture, color and so forth.

Morris agrees with the other dancer-writers: the study of music is basic to the study of dance because rhythm, their common feature, links them. Students learn to respond quickly in their rhythm-training classes. Morris's students also compose their own percussion scores, songs, and poems to accompany their dances. They learn note values, how to count simple and complex rhythms, and how to write musical scores. They sing art songs and folk songs. When they interpret the same piece of music, they see how each dancer creates a different interpretation. The study of music and painting enables students to apply the principles—emphasis, contrast, repetition, harmony, accentuation—of one art to the others. These combine to give a unique *treatment* to each work of art. This understanding of the principles of good "treatment" in a work of art is similar to Jaques-Dalcroze's statement in his essay, "Music and the Dancer" (1919): "we have the right to demand from dancers that elements of musical phrasing, shading, time, and dynamics should be observed by them" (Jaques-Dalcroze, 1921:297). Other ideas of Morris also reflect her knowledge of Dalcroze principles.

Only Moller and Morris introduce improvisation in their discussions of composing dances. With her concept of free exploration of movement, Morris identifies dance as more equal with music than do the others. She also integrates the creative study of the plastic arts with dance and music composition. Without any philosophic or aesthetic explanation, she trusts that composition in arts shares common principles (mentioned above)—and she teaches them. Composer and conductor Eugene Goosens taught the music classes at her school when she first founded it. He drew pictures, she explains, of the rhythms and melodies of the music he taught the children. Artist J. D. Fergusen (who became Morris's husband) taught the painting and drawing classes, and he, too, demonstrated how the principles of painting and drawing applied to dance composition.

According to all our authors, music, the twin art of dance, plays a significant part in dancing. For Isadora Duncan, Margaret H'Doubler, and Mary Beegle, it serves as the primary harmonizing factor in creative dancing. Costume design, the other art these three consider in detail, is based on the basic Greek tunic, or something equally simple, which allows the dancer's body complete unbound freedom. Though Isadora Duncan's students studied all the arts, Morris describes her curricular goals for each art in more detail. Of equal importance to evolving a method to teach composition and performance for these three dancer-writers is their formulation of specific exercise systems to enable their dancers to dance with control, fluidity, and spontaneous naturalness. The next chapter presents the background of their creation of exercise systems and discusses the systems each dancer-writer evolved.

6
Exercise Systems and Technique for Dancing

Isadora and Raymond Duncan, Helen Moller, Margaret Morris, and Margaret H'Doubler evolved exercise systems to help train their dancers in the art of dancing. By considering their exercise systems in the context of education, physical education, and recreation in the early part of this century, we can better see why they invented them. In the first place, they followed the lead of their rival, ballet, where students studied a sequence of traditional techniques which systematically trained a dancer to dance ballet. Secondly, at the end of the 1700s and the beginning of the 1800s, experts in several European countries developed sequences of exercises called "gymnastics" primarily for military training because newly formed citizen armies began conscripting men whom they found seriously out of shape and thus ill-prepared to fight a war. Educators then adopted these exercise systems to train students in public schools and clubs. The exercises in these sequences followed one another in a methodical and prescribed manner, with a predetermined order and stated number of repetitions. Proponents brought the German and Swedish gymnastic systems to England and the United States. Also, experts incorporated other systems of exercise into physical education activities, among them the Delsartian and Dalcroze systems, which grew out of theater and music training respectively. Today's American students in their physical education classes continue to practice similar training sequences but call them "calisthenics" or "physical fitness" programs. The rationale behind the gymnastic training in the 1700s and 1800s parellels the motivation for contemporary physical fitness programs: to improve health for personal well-being and to build strength to insure a person's protective and defensive capability. Leaders among the "natural" dancers borrowed exercises from the available systems and adapted them for their purposes, especially from the Delsarte and Dalcroze training methods.

In *Movement Education: Its Evolution and a Modern Approach* (1969), Margaret C. Brown and Betty K. Sommer explain the French response to the competing systems practiced in France at the end of the nineteenth century and the beginning of the twentieth. Though advocates promoted the German and the Swedish systems for military training, a group of French experts wanted "to create a national system that 'would emphasize self-expression by harmonious movements, grace and utility'" (Brown and Sommer, 1969:24; quote R. Tait McKenzie, *Exercise in Education and Medicine*. Philadelphia: W.B. Saunders, Company, 1923). Two men led the evolution of this expressive style of gymnastic exercise: Etienne Jules Marey (1830-1904) and Georges Demeny (1850-1917). Professor Marey taught applied physiology at the Sorbonne. During this time of the development of industrial machinery Marey became fascinated by the mechanics of human movement. He wrote *La Machine Animale* (1873), based on his studies of animal and human movement. His student Georges Demeny continued his teacher's systematic study of animals and humans, using the new photographic action techniques developed by Eadweard Muybridge (1830-1904). Besides laboratory study, Demeny based his work on his own gymnastic experience and his studies of physical training in ancient Greece. Brown and Sommer describe his understanding of movement as:

> a manifestation of life and [the understanding] that the stimulation to movement could be either external or internal, mental or emotional. In particular, his study of the motion of animals and birds convinced him that movement was not stiff or angular, but round; it was not jerky, but rather continuous, flowing out from the body in all directions and planes in conical or spiral form or in figures of eight. (Brown and Sommer, 1969:25 quote Ernest Loise, *Les Bases Psychologiques de l'Éducation Physique*. Éditions Bourrelier; Paris: Librairie Armand Colin, 1955: 71-76)

The "naturalistic" system of gymnastics credited to Demeny, developed by Paul Souriau in *The Aesthetics of Movement*, (Paris: Alcan, 1889), probably influenced Raymond and Isadora Duncan as well as Delsarte and Dalcroze.

Just as the dancer-teachers found they needed exercise systems to train their students to dance, physical trainers have long utilized dancing practices to improve grace, flexibility, and rhythmic coordination in their movement activities. During the first third of this century, dancing had advocates from several disciplines: medicine, such as Luther Gulick, M.D. who helped put folk dancing into the elementary school curriculum in the United States; leaders in sports, physical education, hygiene, and dance. These experts identified the value of dancing in the history of physical education, explained its benefits, and justified its inclusion in daily practice. Surprisingly, for a long time sports and physical education evolved separately. Sports activity was popular in English Public Schools (i.e., elite private schools) as an extra-curricular activity where students engaged in little physical education.

In 1920 two Y.M.C.A. physical education instructors, S.C. Staley and D. M. Lowery (S. and L.), wrote a *Manual of Gymnastic Dancing* in which they summarize the history of dancing within physical education. Their survey starts with Ancient Greece. They quote from the essay "Greek Athletic Sports and Festivals" by historian E. Norman Gardiner. He claimed that exercises and simplified dances performed to music played an important part in the training of warriors. Stacey and Lowery trace the use of the Greek "Pyrrhiche" (usually pyrrhic, victory) dance (S. and L., 1920:4) in Ancient Rome and Medieval Europe. Passing through the time of the "Ascetic Ideal," they praise the medieval physician Hieronymus Mercurialis (1530–1606) who recommends dancing in his *De Arts Gymnastica*, "for the physical good it rendered" (S. and L., 1920:5), and they commend Montaigne (1533–1592) because he espouses physical activity of all kinds including dancing. Because philosophers Richard Mulcaster (1530–1611) and John Locke (1632–1714), among others, also recommend dancing as a fine form of physical activity, Staley and Lowery conclude that authorities held dancing in high esteem during the 1600s and 1700s. Educator Johann Basedow (1723-1790) established the physical education program based on Rousseau's educational principles in the famous school, the Philanthropinum, built in the Duchy of Anhalt in Germany. There Basedow introduced dancing to teach the children the quality of gentility, a common function of dance training. Ballroom dance classes for the upper class had always included instruction in deportment, or proper manners, especially for gentlemen interacting with the "weaker" sex; dance manuals routinely contained a section on polite behavior at a ball.

The physical educator, Gut Muths (1759-1839), the grandfather of modern gymnastics, became famous for establishing the German Turner Society. Known as *turnverein* in Germany, turners belonged to gymnastic clubs where they regularly practiced the exercise sequences evolved by Muths. He strongly advocated dancing:

> Dancing is an exercise strongly deserving recommendation as it tends to unite gracefulness and regularity of motion with strength and agility.... A good gymnastic dance for the open air, approaching the heroic ballet for young men and boys, calculated to exercise their strength and ability, excite innocent mirth and youthful heroism and cherish their love of country through the accompaniment of song, is an extremely desirable object which is still wanting among all our improvements in the art.

(Staley and Lowery, 1920:6-7)

Muth discusses the major ideals to be accomplished in "play," a new notion which thinkers of the late 1800s began to consider as a crucial part of human life: strength, agility, mirth, innocence, love of country—all in nature's fresh air.

The two originators of the major gymnastic exercise systems used for military training are Friedrich L. Jahn (1778-1852), who developed Muth's Turnverein system into the worldwide program, and Pehr H. Ling (1776-1839), who developed the famous Swedish Gymnastic system which uses many pieces of apparatus commonly found in gymnasia today. Jahn and Ling did not concern themselves with dancing because they intended their systems to increase the fitness level among the ill-prepared military recruits who fought in the wars during the first half of the 1800s. Other countries, including the United States, adapted these two competing systems: the Swedish system depends on apparatus, while the German one uses "free exercises" in which participants manipulate (swing in circles) small hand-held objects such as duck pins, balls, and hoops. Experts in the Scandinavian and later the Eastern European countries transformed these systems into "Rhythmic Gymnastics."

Less well known nineteenth-century leaders incorporated dance-related activities into their physical education practices: Francisco Amaros (1789-1848), whose work in France developed the circus-like apparatus of trapeze and rings; Adolph Spiess (1810-1858), who is credited with introducing the Roundel, a series of marching, hopping, skipping, and running movements and their variations; Gustave Hamilton (1827), in England who mentions dancing as valuable but not part of the exercise "order of the day"; Catharine Esther Beecher (1800-1878), who founded normal schools (teachers colleges) in the United States where women's gymnastics incorporated elementary dance activities; Dr. Dioclesian Lewis, who derived his system of *New Gymnastics for Men, Women, and Children* (1862) from the European systems and included hopping, skipping, leaping, running, and the change step to musical accompaniment; and Eberhard (1887), who called the folk dances he introduced into the turners' routines, "Fancy Steps" (S. and L., 1920:8-14).

Dr. W. G. Anderson originated actual gymnastic dancing. Dancing, Anderson claimed, would arouse greater interest in gymnastics. He taught steps and sequences of jigs, reels, clogs, breakdowns, ballet, buck-and-wing, and soft shoe to all his classes in the Brooklyn Normal School of Gymnastics, in Chautauqua, and at Yale University at the turn of the century. Dr. Claes J. Enebuske (1890) included his version of gymnastic dancing within the "day's order" in the Boston

School of Gymnastics, as did H.B. Gilbert (1894) in Harvard Summer School of Physical Education. O. L. Hebbert and W. J. Davison popularized gymnastic dancing in the Y.M.C.A. programs, bringing dancing to a large number of laypeople outside the normal schools, colleges, and special gymnastic training centers.

Competing ideas about the value of physical education (or "physical training" or "physical culture") in American and European education created a minor war among the systems. Either physical education leaders advocated one system which emphasized strength, endurance, and toughness, or another which developed flexibility, coordination, and an awareness of skillful movement. Staley and Lowery's advocacy of gymnastic dancing exemplifies their educational values. Supporters of dancing as part of physical training value individuality over conformity, agility over strength, freedom over power, play over work, rhythmicity over endurance.

Educators influenced the originators of each gymnastic system; their philosophical or educational ideas reflected current knowledge about the physical development of children or adults. For instance, Rousseau's ideas about play, the child's relationship to his or her body, and education in a natural setting influenced Basedow. The ideas about individual development and a curriculum based on the child's needs and interests propounded by Johann Pestalozzi (1746-1827), and his student Friedrich Froebel (1782-1852), influenced German physical educator Philipp Von Fellenberg (1771-1844). Fellenberg introduced gardening, swimming, dancing, music, and other physical activities into traditional formal education for the upper classes in Germany (Hackensmith, 1966). Each gymnastic system reflected a philosophic attitude about education, an understanding of the human body, and a selection of the best activities for people to do.

In her *Innovators and Institutions in Physical Education* (1971), Ellen Gerber lists Francois Delsarte and Emile Jaques-Dalcroze among the innovators of important "systems" of exercise programs. Though Delsarte evolved his exercises to improve the emotional depth of actor's gestures, and Dalcroze worked out his exercises to enable musicians' interpretations of the music to be more fluid and rhythmic, their students and followers formalized their teachers' instructions into systems of exercise and adapted them to physical training situations of all kinds, private and public, educational and recreational. These exercise systems competed with the other physical training systems during the first quarter of the twentieth century. For example, Leslie Clendenen in *The Art of Dancing: Its Theory and Practice*, published in successive printings between

1903 to 1919, offers instructions to carry out "The Dalcroze Principles of Eurhythmics" and *attitudes* for "Pantomime and Dramatic Posture Dance" (Delsartian positions) (see Plate 58). As a dance teacher Clendenen included these systems along with ballet, pantomime, Egyptian, Greek, and "Esthetic and Rhythmic" dancing which he introduced on page 61 but called "Interpretive and Nature Dance" on page 63 (Clendenen, 1919). In the 1919 edition of Clendenen's book he claims that the American National Dance Teachers Association adopted his book as their official training manual.

This long summary of the relationship between physical education and dance clarifies that during the first thirty years of the twentieth century early modern dance, which had it seeds in the revival of Greek dance, Delsartian expression, Dalcroze's eurhythmic training, and pageantry, fit into a larger picture where physical activity—exercise systems, sports, games, hiking in nature, and dancing—was seen as a way to improve one's health, well-being, patriotic feelings, spirit, and life. By doing these good activities people's lives would improve and thus society would flourish. Or so thought the radical utopians, the progressive educators, the religious leaders, the social workers, the physical educators, and the dancers who preached this gospel, especially if the activities took place outdoors in nature. And the innovators of "natural" dance joined the other advocates of exercise in formulating a system of exercises which they taught to their students.

In her discussion of technique, Isadora Duncan refers to gymnastic exercises which ready the body for dancing. These exercises do not resemble the acrobatic exercises used for training today's gymnasts for competition on the balance beam, parallel bars, and floor routines for Olympic-style gymnastics. The gymnastic exercises to which Duncan refers more likely derive from Delsartian ones and the popular French naturalistic gymnastics she found in use in Europe. Irma Duncan, one of Isadora's adopted daughters, who taught in her schools in Berlin and Russia, explains Isadora's "Gymnastics" as Lesson No. XII in her little book, *The Technique of Isadora Duncan* (1937):

> For any one who considers taking up the study of our dancing it is necessary to do at least some gymnastics every day. . . . First there are exercises at the bar to relax and limber the legs. Secondly, exercises to relax and limber the body. Thirdly, exercises for the development of elasticity in the ankles. The latter exercise is extremely important. (Duncan, 1937:31)

She instructs readers to swing one leg up in front, to the side, and to the back. Then rise on to the toes and bend the knees, keeping the heels together, and descend slowly, keeping the spine straight. Bending the torso forward, sideways, and back follows. Repeat these directions with the head, and lastly, move the hips to each side and then in a rotary motion without moving the shoulders. This exercise for the hips sheds another light on Isadora's verbal, written opposition to using the pelvis; she does not omit it when preparing her dancers to dance. Most gymnastic systems of the day included variations of these warm-up exercises.

In her writings, Isadora Duncan frequently comments about dance technique from a positive as well as negative point of view. She understands dance technique, as a means to an end (Duncan, 1928:81) and not an end in itself as in ballet, or in the other current systems of Swedish Gymnastics or Dalcroze Eurhythmics (Duncan, 1928:101). These systems, she warns, kill the body's natural movement abilities. To develop the body's strength and flexibility requires some special gymnastic exercises. Isadora believes these must be done daily before beginning to dance. These exercises should prepare the body to express itself in harmonious and natural motions. Then every fiber becomes sensitively alert and responsive to the melody and flow of nature (Duncan, 1928:81). As one of the preparatory techniques she uses plain walks in simple rhythms, first slowly, then quickly, and adds more complex rhythms as the students progress in their classes. (Jaques-Dalcroze espouses this same technique in his teaching and writing around 1912.) The other dancer-writers studied here also utilize this format of loosely structured rhythmic movement training.

In Isadora's technique training, the walks lead to a series of movement themes and variations based on emotions, such as fear or sorrow. In her training sequence she includes great strides, leaps, and bounds with lifted forehead and far-spread arms (Duncan, 1928:52). Teachers in a modern dance classes of today continue to follow this sequence of walks, runs, and then leaps. But Isadora sets the standard of achievement when she claims that movement should be light as a flame (Duncan, 1928:101). Even violence, she coaches, gains power if done with restraint. The teacher must adjust these techniques to fit the developmental level of children, adolescents, and adults (Duncan, 1928:81). These daily exercises make the body as perfect an instrument as possible so that harmony of self-discovered natural dancing can permeate it completely.

Isadora sets rigor and precision as her standard for technique. Though in her dancing she gave the impression of being free and spontaneous, in fact her methods of training and composition required careful planning and regular practice. The language in which she describes her goals for dance technique resembles most of her writing on other topics, but when she discusses her technique itself, she uses fewer metaphors and offers specific examples, such as leaps, bounds, outstretched arms. Though Isadora accepted the responsibility of writing as part of her career and wrote eloquently, her choice of physical words, in this instance, stands out in her essays and hints at her dancing genius.

Raymond Duncan's discussion of his technique system reflects the ideas of the exercise theorists he encountered in France. The happy-machine metaphor he uses to explain the body contrasts greatly with the reasons for studying natural movement: harmonious exercises provide a spiritual experience to which everyone is entitled. Current gymnastic systems, Raymond complains, neglect the true spirit of exercise. Their innovators claim they base their systems on the games of ancient Greece, but in ancient Greece, argues Raymond, they expressed classical emotions, precision, and beauty. Today's participants seem only to be interested in the external qualities of muscular strength, speed, and distance. The word, "physical," Raymond reminds his readers, means nature, and "physical culture" means the cultivation of the entire human being. In exercise, muscles and intelligence participate together. The best system of gymnastic, he stresses, must be based on natural movements which come from natural activities: normal work and games. These ideas echo Demeny's.

In the first part of his essay Raymond introduces the goals and qualities of naturalistic gymnastics. In the second part he recounts experiences from his life to illustrate how and why he formulated his system of gymnastic exercises. He tells of not wanting to sit still in school; learning how to send telegraph messages, an activity which actively employs one hand; working in a print shop and using two hands; hiking across mountains and rivers, thus, finally using his entire body. His search for satisfying bodily involvement within his life's activities, he explains, led him to study things Greek in museums where, in his mind's eye, he collected enough Greek movement to imagine it in action cinematographically. After his study of Greek designs and movements, he watched farmers and skilled workers of many kinds. He saw them radiating joy and health and recognized the similarities between the movements on the Greek vases and the natural movements of skilled workers.

When Raymond discusses the study of gymnastic exercises, his choice of words shifts from machine images to spiritual ideals, reflecting his unified vision of human beings in nature.

And if we undertake a study of gymnastics, it is not only because we wish to increase or conserve our energies, because we desire that all the parts of our bodies, and all our organs constitute a human harmony, but because we want above all to put ourselves in harmony with the movements of our soul, which is itself in direct contact with the divine movement, in order to truly understand, and to fulfill our task in the universe well. (Duncan, 1914:5)

His definition of "harmony" with the movements of our "soul" connected to the "divine" movement of the universe embodies a profound aesthetic goal for his gymnastic exercises and reflects the spiritualism espoused by Theosophists. These words convey a goal that goes beyond Raymond's concept of a happy machine-like body working efficiently, for he connects human actions to the workings of the universe and the unknown power that drives that action.

Raymond bases his system of movement on expressive not decorative ancient designs. Movement, he insists, only appears curved or undulating. In contrast to Isadora's idea of the wave, his observations of movement led him to understand it as a series of angles. All design and therefore movement is built on triangles inscribed in squares. He based his natural gymnastics on angular movement and claims that from this system of movements, the art of harmonious dance can be built. In her pamphlet, Eleanor Elder describes exactly how to perform Raymond's six fundamental Greek positions (see Plates 62-65).

Unlike Raymond Duncan and most of the others discussed in this book, Beegle does not work out an original system of technique. Beegle believes the creative aspect of dance makes it a living art, not one, like ballet, that only passes on its traditional techniques and content from the past. Like all arts, natural dancing, she asserts, has technique as its foundation, but its technique differs from former concepts because dance "is a living, growing thing, passing continually from one form to another" (Beegle and Crawford, 1916:195). "In natural dancing, which has to evolve its own technique," she asserts, "steps are studied as functions of the fundamental movements of the body, together with the mental states, or emotions, to which they correspond. As a foundation for the study of bodily movements expressing emotions, four elements are recognized . . . walking, running, leaping and twirling" (Beegle and Crawford, 1916:210). Beegle instructs the dance director to let the dancers explore the range of each of these locomotor movements by changing their mood, tempo, and accent to find the best way to communicate the dramatic emotion of the dance.

Each dance session should begin with a warm-up which Beegle describes as a systematic routine of exercises that form "the foundation of every rehearsal" (Beegle and Crawford, 1916:222). These exercises train the body for control and range of expression. After dancers learn them, the dance director should encourage dancers to experiment and dance them in several different moods.

Beegle reflects her Dalcroze training, seeing rhythm as the central controlling force in the pageant, when insisting that elementary exercises in rhythm must be included in each session: "The elements of rhythm include instruction in such simple ideas as time, note values, accent and simple phrasing" (Beegle and Crawford, 1916:224). Walking, running, leaping, and twirling first should be tried simply on the beat and then in two-four, four-four, six-eight, and three-four time, until the dancers acquire a feeling for and response to each rhythm.

Like Beegle, Moller values improvisation. Though even dancing for Moller remains primarily improvisatory, throughout her book she articulates detailed instructions for actual dance technique. In her definition of dance, not dancing, she states in Delsartian terms the primary goal of her style of technical dance training: "Dance is the art of rhythmic balance and that perfect co-operation of the muscles which results in graceful and harmonious movements" (Moller, 1918:55). "Graceful" is a word she repeats many times, along with "lightness," "soaring," "vigorous," and "beautiful," but not "mechanical," when she describes her style of dancing. Instructions include: The body is balanced, like Greek statues, on one bare foot which remains flat while the other rises on half toe directly next to it. This posture allows one hip and shoulder to tip down while maintaining the body in a symmetrical arrangement. Dancers must involve the entire body in all dancing. To reach the Greek ideal, total body training must create symmetrical proportion in strength and grace. To achieve this end, Moller surmises, the Greeks eliminated any techniques which strengthened one part of the body more than any other.

Running, the most beneficial exercise human beings can do, plays a crucial part in Moller's form of dancing. When her dancers run, they must soar, the feet buoyantly spurning the earth. She identifies the hygienic benefits of this form of exercise: dancers will feel alert, remain unfatigued, stand tall, and exude health and well-being. While explaining benefits of this free and vigorous movement experience, especially for young women, she comments on the unsound restrictions of current child-rearing practices for girls, who must stop active play when they become young women.

In the captions of her photographs, Moller affirms the physical and emotional goals of her natural dancing. It involves the entire body, and the dancers concentrate, physically and emotionally. When commenting on the dancers' facial expressions, she points out how they portray the story or react to a situation in their dancing. "All true physical expression has its generative center in the region of the heart, the same as the emotions which actuate it" (Moller, 1918:96). The words she chooses to describe the facial expressions and bodily positions in the photographs—"open," "free," "gentle," "pleasurable," and above all, "charming"—highlight the positive regenerative emotions which she encourages in her teaching.

Like Moller, H'Doubler evolved a series of exercises for her students; she describes them as scientific. By "scientific" she means based on empirical physiological principles. Technique, she insists, must follow the laws of bodily motion, or "natural movement," found in the study of anatomy, kinesiology, and physics. Both H'Doubler's early books concentrate on exercises she calls "movement fundamentals." Neither the exercises nor her explanations vary or develop much from her first to her second book. The exercises to prepare the body for dancing, she asserts, should develop the greatest range of flexibility which allows complete range of movement in the joint-muscular mechanism. These techniques should "be simple enough to learn in a short amount of time and complex enough to be interesting and valuable to students for whom dance is an art" (DPE, 1925:33). They must make the body "capable of being sensitive and responsive to the demands made upon it" (MD, 1921:8). By this she means that the techniques will establish such sound habits of muscular control that when students dance to music in response to their feelings, their bodies will be expressive without conscious thought. These techniques, movement fundamentals, she reminds her readers, are not dancing. She intends them to develop "harmonious functioning not only [for] all the parts of the body but to no small extent, all the parts of the body and mind as well" (DPE, 1925:57). For H'Doubler dancing as an educational activity serves the whole person: the mind and the body.

In her theoretical discussion of technique H'Doubler offers detailed physical goals: movement must be made clear, from its source to its follow through; it must come to a climax without obstruction; it must be phrased in an orderly manner and come to rest with an ease of effort. The exercise sequence starts on the floor so the beginning student does not need to contend with gravity. She designed the exercises to train first the big muscles which control the spine so as to coordinate it smoothly in a folding and unfolding action (flexion and extension), before developing the smaller movements of the limbs (see Plate 85). Following the standing exercises, the students travel through space running, hopping, skipping, leaping, galloping, and sliding. H'Doubler explains the order in which to do the movements and suggests how students should carry them out: with complete mental absorption and no self-consciousness. The students' freedom and joy in moving, gained in the study of dance, she predicts, will carry into other realms of life. Her attitude foreshadows the underlying purpose of this creative art experience, to elevate students' lives to a higher level.

Like H'Doubler, Eleanor Elder believes dance students must systematically prepare their bodies to dance. The techniques best suited for accomplishing these goals, Elder declares, are not found in military-style drills and exercises but are available in methods such as "Eurhythmics" of M. Jaques-Dalcroze. Here she disagrees with Isadora Duncan and Mary Beegle who do not recommend the Dalcroze series of exercises. Elder describes the students schooled in this system as being sensitive, alert, quick, and able to move instantly in response to the most complex rhythm. Though the training exercises of Dalcroze are not dancing, Elder suggests that they might "in time amalgamate with some of the schools of natural dancing, and in that case the value of both systems will be tremendously increased" (Elder, 1918:5). The stream of natural dance training created by Mary Beegle, Gertrude Colby, and Margaret H'Doubler appears to have carried out this suggestion by Elder.

In her essay Elder concentrates on the Greek style of natural dancing which does not deny "the laws of nature and gravity" (Elder, 1918:5) the way ballet does. Recently Isadora and Raymond Duncan have revived this style of dancing. Elder praises Isadora's performances for introducing natural dancing to a wide audience and changing the Russian Ballet leaders' view of the potential of ballet.

> Few people realise to what an extent Miss Duncan affected the world, or that it is to her that we owe the wonderful Russian Ballet of the pre-war days, as seen in London and Paris. M. Mikail Fokine, a director of the Imperial Ballet School in Petrograd, after seeing Isadora Duncan dance, asked her to give a special performance in the Ballet School. From that time there was a definite split in the academy, a group of students breaking away from the old ballet and introducing her methods into their own art. Amongst these we find such names as Pavlova, Karsavina, Nidjinsky [sic], Mordkin and Volinine Bohm, and many others, and it was these artists that gave us the Russian Ballet as we know it to-day. (Elder, 1918:6)

This detail about Duncan's role in the revolution in Russian Ballet is not commonly found in today's dance history books, though other authors mention it in books of that time. Though Isadora had major impact on dance, it is Raymond, Elder claims, who systematized the method of teaching the Greek dancing which "is in harmony with nature" and insures that "every movement is sincere in its expression" (Elder, 1918:6).

Elder describes how Raymond Duncan identified the "law of balance" (to which Moller repeatedly refers) and implemented it into the six fundamental positions on which he bases his natural dancing techniques. This "balance" refers to the natural opposition of the right arm to the left leg when human beings walk, run, and move in space. Dancers perform these six positions and the dancing in which they use these positions, in profile. When dancers do not face the audience, they do not experience self-consciousness. Elder claims that these positions will "be excellent exercises for the body, giving balance and poise as well as a good all round development of the muscles" (Elder, 1918:17). All dancing in this natural Greek system is done on the balls of the feet. Whereas Raymond held rigidly to these laws, some of his students, reports Elder, such as Miss Spong in her school in Hamstead and Margaret Morris in her school in Chelsea, developed these fundamentals more freely and applied them success-fully in many educational settings.

Elder gives more detail about Morris's techniques when she reviews the curriculum of Morris's school: "The classes are varied with marching, Greek exercises and dances of the simplest type, that are more in the nature of games or plays acted to music, in which the expression of various emotions is called into play" (Elder, 1918:11). Students interpret these techniques in numerous ways. Her instructions echo those of Mary Beegle.

In her book *Margaret Morris Dancing*, Morris explains the goals of her technique system and the educational basis of the training she offers in her school. She believes her exercises are fundamental; because she bases her exercise system on movements natural to all people—walking, running, hop-ping, and jumping—and people of all ages can do them and will benefit from them. She enlarged these vigorous movements by accentuating their range of movement. They require counterbalancing the upper body with the lower body, thus, they involve the entire body. She identifies this balance as the principle of "opposition" (Morris, 1926:16). The principle of opposition is one of the three basic principles of the Delsarte System of Expression. Raymond and Isadora Duncan were well acquainted with this system of exercises from their early days performing in theaters in America (Ruyter, 1979:ch. 2). Although the move-ments in Morris's exercise system can be seen on Greek vase paintings, she claims to have seen the same movements depicted in Egyptian and Cambodian art. She describes their benefit:

> At any rate, I have found them to be of extraordinary value in physical development, and exactly what was needed, being actually an *accentuation* of normal walking and running positions, but with the necessary fixing of postures essential to the education of the muscles. They accentuate the turn at the waist, the bend of the knees, and by using more definite and strong positions of the arms, use the shoulder and back muscles, so that the holding of these positions induces, by building up the necessary muscles, an easy and balanced walk, and correct posture in standing. (Morris, 1926:17)

Morris's physical analysis of her technique concentrates on the actual muscular results of her training. Her system includes more movements than those based just on Greek paintings: leg lifting, twisting, stretching, bending. These movements too are natural; she encourages those students who can perform acrobatic positions to do them. Several of the photographs show students kneeling on one leg while pulling the heel of the other foot backwards toward their heads in an extreme acrobatic position (see Plate 21). This example demonstrates what Morris means when she explains that "natural" is a relative term.

Morris summarizes the tenets of her system of physical culture by claiming:

> –That it includes all that is necessary for the development of healthy intelligent human beings.
> –That it requires no special conditions.
> –That it is absorbingly interesting.
> –That it is suitable for people of all ages from two years, as the exercises can be graduated to suit any age, or state of physical fitness or weakness.
> –That is is directly applicable to ordinary life, causing people to walk and stand well, to breathe properly to move freely and easily, at the same time training the mind in concentration and construction. (Morris, 1926:29)

Her system, she asserts, also offers sound training for professional dancers by providing the essentials of dance training—balance, suppleness, and agility. Like the other writers in this study, Morris views ballet technique as limiting because it is artificial, rigid, and mechanical, and it cannot convey "*new* forms of movement and design" (Morris, 1926:50). Her MMM, as she called her system, served professional athletes; physicians who prescribed it for their patients called it "land swimming" because it benefits the body as much as does swimming.

The technique systems which our dancer-writers developed share basic organizing characteristics: they are simple and easily learned; they are natural, unlike ballet; they are "harmonious," that is, they fit the body easily and spiritually; and they are based upon the body's daily activities of walking, running, and so forth. From the pictures and descriptions in their books, the systems have physical features in common: parallel feet, enlarged though everyday movement, and oppositional balance. Unlike the technique systems developed by dancers in the 1930s, 1940s, and 1950s, these early ones, for the most part did not derive from artistic dance activity where choreographers produced dances in a repertoire. They intended technique training to increase students' physical well-being and give them the experience of dancing, which took priority over making finished dances.

Each system also has the stamp of the individual who developed it. The vocabulary used to describe these "fundamental" exercises, the goals and ways of training—using rhythmic variations as a basic way to enlarge the range of movement experience of the dancers—relate closely to the work and words of Isadora and Raymond Duncan. Evidence of the Duncan influence continues in several other areas of this newly emerging dance form as will be seen in the discussion of education in the next chapter.

7
Dance Education

Many of the dancer-writers I examine in this book espouse progressive educational philosophy because its proponents challenged traditional school curricula, favored what they called "natural" education, and saw educational value in the arts by recognizing the contribution the arts make to children's learning. One of the earliest spokespersons for natural education was Jean-Jacques Rousseau (1712-1778). Progressive educators quoted his ideas about the arts to buttress their argument that education should develop the "whole" child. The dancer-writers agreed with the value Rousseau placed on movement education: "Children," Rousseau observed, "are always in motion; a sedentary life is injurious" (Dewey, 1916:115). Rousseau's ideas verified their own basic instincts; his stature as a respected philosopher emboldened them to assert their belief in the value of the arts in a child's education.

Active experience in all the arts underlies Isadora Duncan's concept of education. Early in her performing career, she established her first school (1904), and twice more she opened schools of dance. Her devotion to the institution of a school as a mechanism for social change and betterment of humanity reflects her radical utopian beliefs. She established her first school before governments enacted child labor laws; thus, students attending her school escaped inadequate schooling, poor living, and oppressive working conditions. She espoused the educational ideas of Rousseau: all children before the age of twelve should gain their understanding of the world only through their senses and not from books (Duncan, 1928:124). In the curriculum of her school she carried out this vision by using the arts—music, poetry, and song— to teach her students how the arts express the feelings of people with grace and beauty (Duncan, 1928:117). In her school, in conjunction with the other arts, students also study dance as an art. Besides the arts, nature serves as the other primary source of knowledge for her students. Classes occur outside whenever possible so the students can receive plenty of light and air (Duncan, 1928:83), improve their health, and have direct contact with live and growing things. After field trips to museums, Duncan reports, the children dance about what they saw (Duncan, 1928:97) and thereby reinforce their learning by expressing it physically and directly.

In the curriculum of Isadora's school, children composed, practiced, and perfected their own solos and group dances. The process of composition was rigorous and careful: "We do not allow the child to make a single movement unless it knows why it makes it" (Duncan, 1928:75). When children perform their dances, she encourages them to invest their movements spontaneously with their own feelings and happiness. Surrounding children with a graceful environment, Isadora believes, contributes to the natural development of their love of beauty. Through the study of arts and nature the children simultaneously become conscious of their individuality and their place in the universe; thus, their study provides them a social education as well as an emotional and intellectual one. Her curriculum objectives and pedagogical methods exemplify radical utopian and romantic concepts about the role of art in education: the arts can improve and elevate human lives.

The dance education Isadora espouses develops the natural abilities of children; because they love to move, it is natural for them to dance. She teaches them to breathe, vibrate, feel, and become one with the harmony and movement in nature (Duncan, 1928:77, 82). She uses daily exercises to reach these ends and makes sure the children enjoy them. The technical training which she describes as a set of gymnastic exercises remains a means to an end. By doing these exercises, Duncan claims, the children will also develop a vitality and a high degree of energy to enable the dance spirit to enter. By "dance spirit" she means creative inspiration which stimulates her students to move freely and spontaneously. Her goal reaches beyond training the muscles of the children; she readies them to express the outpouring of their souls.

Duncan delineates what dance education must exclude. None of the current dance activities—bodily culture, Swedish gymnastics, Dalcroze Eurhythmics, or ballet—are appropriate for children (Duncan, 1928:49). She views the activities of ballet as especially wrong. Children should not be forced to execute unnatural movement or imitate nymphs, fairies, or courtesans (Duncan, 1928:49). No system yet established is adequate. Echoing Rousseau, Duncan believes that only a child's unique nature must guide their dance education (Duncan, 72). Here Duncan's ideas reflect the romantic notion that all children are potential artists; they only need freedom and encouragement to evolve into artists capable of expressing the universal rhythms in nature and the ecstasy in their souls.

Isadora's brother Raymond agrees with the educational principles his sister articulates; his educational model goes beyond Rousseau. In the kindergartens of Friedrich Froebel (1782-1852), Raymond points to the high status of dance and gymnastics; children must learn little songs, dances, and games because when they become adults this experience can enable them to generate great emotions and be capable of sensing great truths. Raymond not only espouses dance for four and five year old children; all students and people should have the opportunity to create their own dances. In contrast, the daily-life motions of city dwellers of his day have become ugly and stupid because the people lack a good movement education. He believes in the necessity of proper movement training for people to live a harmonious life.

Like Isadora Duncan, Mary Beegle's book disseminates child-centered educational goals while setting high standards for dance composition and performance even in the context of a pageant. The affirmative tone of Beegle's instructions reflects her pedagogical values. She suggests how the director should offer only positive criticism to the dancers. He or she must encourage dancers to relax their feet, since a pointed foot is reminiscent of ballet. Instructors must continuously foster creativity. After the dancers learn their dances, the director might continue developing the dancers' expressive abilities by having them execute their dances in moods not in the pageant. Agreeing with Isadora Duncan, Beegle asserts that this creative expression requires discipline: "The dance is a clear expression of an idea; it may not be vague or indefinite" (Beegle and Crawford, 1916:230). Even the solo dancers need to understand that every movement must be "carefully calculated to make plain to the audience the meaning" (Beegle and Crawford, 1916:233). Beegle values positive encouragement; this helps the dancers perform expressive, non-balletic dance movements clearly and precisely.

In contrast to the emphasis on performance by Beegle and Isadora Duncan, H'Doubler uses the historical and cultural background of dance primarily to underscore its educational value, her major emphasis. Dancing ought to be "an educational activity, instead of an outer acquisition of simulated grace" (MD, 1921:7). This sentence contains two of the three divisions into which H'Doubler separates dance: dance science, the art of dancing, and dancing as an art. "Simulated grace" describes the art of dancing, the professional skill-driven form. "An educational activity" fits into the category of dancing as an art, since in this category dancing is "genuinely expressive of the inner man" (DPE, 1925:8). Dance science encompasses the study of dance movement through anatomy and kinesiology.

Self-expression of emotions underlies most of H'Doubler's educational goals and characterizes the ideals of progressive education where education "draws out" the students and develops their "physical, mental, spiritual and social needs" (DPE, 1925:29). Though each student is unique, as a group, the students share much in common; they need to be able to express their "emotional reaction to life" in an art form (DPE, 1925:33). Most importantly, she asserts, they need to learn to discriminate between the higher and lower forms of entertainment and recreation as well as be prepared for the "graver undertakings of life" (DPE, 1925:5). For H'Doubler, Greek civilization provides the model for the higher forms of entertainment. In this context, dance achieves the goals H'Doubler wants to achieve. Dance

> helps to develop the body, to cultivate the laws and appreciation of beauty, to stimulate the imagination and challenge the intellect, to deepen and refine the emotional life and to broaden the social capacities of the individual that he may profit from and serve the greater world without. (DPE, 925:33)

Here H'Doubler identifies how dancing satisfies the physical, mental, spiritual, and social needs of students. This educational model values public service as well; schooling must prepare students to participate in a democracy.

H'Doubler particularizes these educational goals in physical and psychological terms. Dancing serves not just a few talented students but gives all students pleasure and exhilaration when they experience rhythmic movement and "exercise all [their] faculties in harmonious self-expression" (DPE, 1925:222). Dancing provides them relaxing recreation where they may release nervous tension; it allows them physical and emotional expression. The real aim of dancing goes beyond the physical; the creative activity develops the students' personalities so they reach the height of their powers. Dance refines their taste, and it strengthens their "preferences for the finer things in art and life" (DPE, 1925:222). After their study of dance, H'Doubler hopes the preferences of her students will widen: "This attitude toward art and life is the greatest contribution of dance to modern education" (DPE, 1925:222). H'Doubler's views here reflect the rational recreationists who wanted to rescue the common people from their wasteful leisure-time activities in bars, music halls, movies, and penny arcades.

H'Doubler's ideas about dance teachers and their teaching center on the life-elevating goal of dancing. This attitude can be seen in her initial statements about teachers in both her early books. In *A Manual of Dancing* she insists that those teaching interpretive dancing should believe in its educational value, "not as a performance but as an educational influence of the finest type" (MD, 1921:12). In *The Dance and Its Place in Education,* she asserts that teachers help people "to find meaning in life and joy in living" (DPE, 1925:6). Her other comments about the qualifications of teachers ring of progressive educational ideals. Teachers must be enthusiastic and devoted experts in dance, knowledgeable about music, and sensitive to the individual needs of each student. Teachers must create an artistic atmosphere, while at the same time they can help diminish shyness and self-consciousness in their students.

In addition to theoretical principles, both of H'Doubler's books contain practical guidelines to help teachers conduct dance classes. These guidelines give the teacher responsibility for balancing the varied parts of the curriculum: movement fundamentals must be balanced with creative work, too much freedom to be imaginative must be balanced with too little freedom, time spent in the process of creating must be balanced with rehearsing for performance, teacher guidance of student work must be balanced with self-guidance, and technical growth must be balanced with creative growth. H'Doubler even suggests what teachers might expect from their beginning students. Students' attempts to compose dance studies, she cautions, may be "crude and naive" at first, but with more experience they will reach a "higher plane of expression" (MD, 1921:10). H'Doubler urges teachers to appreciate these first creative inventions even in their earliest and most primitive stage. Do not focus on the external results. The goal remains to develop taste and appreciation of the good and beautiful in art and life; these experiences, she hopes, may bear fruit in future years (DPE, 1925:55). H'Doubler's educational goals emphasize the creative process over the performed product, focus on long term goals, and assume that all students have creative ability which she can readily tap.

Though Margaret Morris integrates performance into her school's curriculum, Eleanor Elder explains how progressive art educational values continue as Morris's primary aim. Morris focuses on the integration of all a student's abilities in daily school experience through developing their six senses. Elder advocates offering creative arts education, like the program in the Margaret Morris school, to all British children, though Elder worries about finding enough teachers to teach this material adequately. The artistic habit of thinking, she argues, must be understood as equal to the scientific and seen as vital in education: "That is what every form of education is working towards—spiritual, mental, emotional and physical expression. The unity of the whole comprises the joy of life" (Elder, 1918:16). These ideas echo H'Doubler's her early writings and most of the other dancer-writers in the present study. The educational program Elder espouses reflects the concept of a unified person. Like our other dancer-writers who discuss educational goals, her ideas reflect the teachings of progressive educators.

Elder calls attention to the educational and artistic value of Morris's notation system which children learn as they practice their exercises and compose their dances. Elder itemizes the curriculum at Morris's school: not only do students study music, they also apply drawing and painting to the costume, set design, and floor plans of their dances. Children, Elder points out, write their own poetic and rhythmic accompaniment for some of their dances. This detailed description of Morris's school, written by Elder eight years before Morris published her first book, corroborates Morris's account of her dance-teaching philosophy and practices.

In *Margaret Morris Dancing*, Morris concentrates on the educational benefits of dancing. She trusts that students can create an infinite variety of dances. She feels strongly that Italian ballet is not the only viable dance technique in which one can compose dances. Her interests lie in creating a new form of dance. The final paragraph in her book eloquently defines the aesthetic goal of her work— to enrich the lives of all:

> Finally, if, as I believe, health and happiness should be the basis for all art—it is reasonable that, to some extent at least, it should become a part of the life of all. There is no reason why average human beings should not develop strong, healthy bodies, and mental and physical control, as well as understanding and appreciation of form, colour and sound, in nature and in art—and in many cases even the power of artistic creation. (Morris, 1926:94)

Like the other dancer-writers discussed in this section, Morris believes dancing and creating dances benefit people's lives, their health, and emotional well-being. The artistic payoff seems an added bonus and only one of the reasons for dancing.

Margaret Morris views notation for dancing as primarily a teaching tool for movement exploration, retention, and study. It makes her teaching easier and helps jog students' memories. The greatest value of notation, Morris asserts, will be to improve dance composition: "In order to write a movement in notation one must analyze it minutely, and would be less likely, in consequence, to compose aimless and stupid movements; and more likely to consider if they were really what was required to convey a particular impression" (Morris, 1926:80). This perceptive observation about the value of dance notation is still being learned by students in today's educational and professional communities.

Because Morris was in the process of preparing a book on her own notation system she only discussed notation briefly. She does present her criteria for a good notation system: it must be useful for all forms of movement and dance to prevent it from becoming outdated; it must be easy to write and read; it must be accurate; most important, it must be universally readable and accepted to insure the continuation of current dance developments. Her interest in notation paralleled Rudolf Laban's who published his first book on movement and dance notation in 1927, a year before Morris's book on dance notation. In the twentieth century several choreographers and dance teachers felt the need to create a notation system for dance. (See Ann Hutchinson-Guest's *Dance Notation: The Process of Recording Dance on Paper*. New York: Dance Horizons, 1984).

Morris writes her book from the point of view of the teacher; throughout, she merges her pedagogical priorities with her aesthetic standards. In some instances she articulates these standards directly. She wants all the movements which her students make to look good:

> Not by an effort to be "graceful"; striving after grace is fatal to good movement, real grace and good looking easy movements can only be the outcome of health and strength. An obvious illustration is the panther or the tiger—remarkable for their wonderfully graceful, easy movements. Such grace is the result of perfectly developed and controlled muscles, and entire freedom from self-consciousness. An analogous grace and confidence in human beings is what I am aiming at. (Morris, 1926:26-27)

Her reference to a tiger or panther is one of the few non-human examples she offers in her many explanations of physical activity. This example also illustrates her understanding of "natural": like Isadora she finds expressive dance movement in the world of animals in nature. Grace, for Morris, comes from strength. This concept counters the late Victorian notion of female ethereal weakness, and it redefines how women can move. Her goal of eliminating self-consciousness echoes an educational goal of Raymond Duncan.

Morris articulates goals for which she strives in her teaching. When children begin to study MMM, she wants them to feel that the exercises are "part of the rhythmic whole" (Morris, 1926:27). By this she means that students must enjoy the exercises and capture their attention. To continue the involvement of the students, she asks them to compose dances. She trains even young children this way: they do age-appropriate techniques, such as walking, running, jumping, and hopping, then they advance to quick and slow rhythms and balancing in held positions. In this way their bodies develop naturally. For professional dancers, the training is more challenging in both technique and composition, but its basis is the same for all her students: to experience naturally graceful movement which they compose or learn from her or from other students.

The study of the arts, Morris believes, benefits everyone. Reflecting Rousseau's vision, she thinks children from the ages of three to twelve should only study the arts and after that age learn more practical skills, such as reading, arithmetic, science, and languages. Echoing Freud, Morris asserts that arts education enables people to express the repressed emotions which develop during their adult life. This early study of movement, color, and sound, she claims, will provide people with ways to express their discontents. Not only will art and movement education benefit people psychologically, it will have physiological value as well. Health will improve with efficient digestion and with increased strength and agility; even some minor physical deformities will be corrected. These values fit with current ideas linking the sciences and the arts together rather than separating parts of reality into separate disciplines. Studying her system, she believes, links the body with the brain and connects people with their surroundings.

Morris's system, she claims, functions for many purposes: educational, theatrical, and recreational. Even professional actors and actresses need to develop their brains beyond the emotional training they receive in the professional theater and they benefit from studying in her program. In the several types of stage entertainments—opera, musical theater, drama, melodrama, and even vaudeville—artistic treatment can improve their quality. Her students become more sensitive to their theatrical and everyday experience. Though she expects to teach some especially talented students, Morris focuses on all people of any age and social class. They will achieve at their own level, she realizes, but everyone should "at least be given the opportunity to develop his capacity to the utmost in every direction" (Morris, 1926:75).

Raymond and Isadora Duncan, Mary Beegle, Margaret H'Doubler, Eleanor Elder, and Margaret Morris share a common educational vision: children are entitled to and benefit from education in the arts at an early age. All of our authors recognize dance as a creative art. The major benefit of dancing, in addition to its creative artistic expression, offers people the opportunity to enhance and preserve life: personally, physically, physiologically, and socially. These experiences elevate one's taste and horizons. That dancing enhances the quality of life reflects the ideas of the rational recreationists who supported the progressive educational movement during the first third of this century in the United States and England.

Our dancer-writers share another feature: their dedication to teaching. They trained other teachers who passed on their ideas to more students. They also sought a formal way to institutionalize their views of dancing and thus established their academies to counteract the power of the established ones. Isadora Duncan, Raymond Duncan, Helen Moller, and Margaret Morris opened private schools of dance. To carry out her radical utopian vision of the role of art in children's education, Isadora Duncan sought public and private support for her students so their schooling would be free. Margaret Morris welcomed students with scholarships in her schools. One can surmise that the same is true for the other school directors mentioned. Mary Beegle and Margaret H'Doubler taught in college and university settings. All our dancer-writers developed dance curricula which had lasting impact on professional and educational dance. The act of institutionalizing their views of dancing in schools, they hoped, would guarantee that their work might continue into the future.

8

Early Twentieth Century
Modern Dance Theory

Before examining the books and photographs, the media by which early twentieth-century modern dancer-writers disseminated their ideas, a synthesis of the theoretical underpinnings of this new dancing-art reveals the dynamic, idealized, and creative basis for what became a recognized academic field and a revitalized artistic profession.

Isadora values dancing to such an extent that she elevates it to the level of a religion. In some of her attempts to define it, we see her fervent belief:

> To dance is to live. (Duncan, 1928:141)

> Man must speak, then sing, then dance. But speaking is the brain, the thinking man. The singing is the emotions, the dancing is the Dionysian ecstasy which carries away all. (Duncan, 1928:139)

> [Dancing] is the movements of the human body in harmony with the movements of the earth. (Duncan, 1928:142)

> For me the dance is not only the art that gives expression to the human soul through movement, but also the foundation of a complete conception of life, more free, more harmonious, more natural. (Duncan, 1928:101)

A close look at these definitions reveals Isadora's theoretical priorities. Each encompasses the activity of dancing, its source in the soul, and its ecstatic emotion, or its feeling of being in harmony with nature. By ecstasy, she means to feel totally unified and free to express honest emotions. The strictures of civilization cut off this sense of freedom and unity; unrestricted, people dancing will synchronize with the rhythms in nature. Dancing, as a metaphor for life, reflects the ups and downs of living; the wave pattern represents the flow, and the ongoingness of dance and life remain constant. Dancing takes precedence over the dancer and the dance. The recurring themes—the soul, harmony, and nature—identified in the discussion of Isadora's views about the body (see

Chapter 4) underpin her theoretical concepts about dance. For her the dancer reveals her soul, dancing requires harmonious movement, and the aesthetic source of the dance lies in nature.

Isadora's praise of dance reflects the radical utopian belief that artists and their arts can elevate and educate the people of the world to live harmoniously, serenely, and peacefully with each other and the earth. Instead of the artist's role as an outside observer of society, radical utopians believe the artist, as part of society, plays a pivotal role in changing the lives of people by means of their art. In Isadora's writing, this romantic and idealized view of the power of the dance to change society may prevent today's readers from recognizing the central features of her theoretical understanding of dance. Her ideas about movement as naturally discovered, technique as a means to an end, composition to express the soul, the aesthetic intent as spiritually illuminating, the aesthetic result of the dance to move the souls of audience members, and its need to reflect the people and the times in which it occurs, stand as a credo of modern dance during the first half of the twentieth century. Many of her contemporary dancer-writers and those who follow this early generation repeat her thoughts, often in similar words.

Raymond agrees with many of Isadora's major conclusions. His ideas about gymnastic exercise and the natural kind of dance they can produce combine the newest scientific and philosophic ideas with the utopian vision of the back-to-nature movement and idealized Greek culture. He expects natural dance to provide people with a way to save themselves from the evils of the city which forces people to engage in ugly expressionless movements. Like Isadora, Raymond sees dancing as a means to achieve a better life. The aesthetic goal of dancing is spiritual and connects human beings with the past and future in the universe. He "preached" this message on the eve of World War I when a unified world seemed far from possible.

As people did in classical Greece, today's arts practitioners, Beegle asserts, must evolve their own art. The integrated arts they perform serve the individual, the community, and the nation by freeing and focussing creative energy for aesthetic purposes. Beegle's ideas about how to compose natural dance and how to teach and coach its dancers sound contemporary and undoubedly serve as a valuable source of current American pedagogical concepts for dance.

Into her hopeful vision of life Moller places her view of the benefits of creative dancing. The dancer must be free of restrictive clothing to move spontaneously and be guided by the basic natural principles of movement. These principles include the use of opposites in both the physical range of movement and emotional expression. The entire body must be vigorously and gracefully involved. Music inspires the dancing which positions of ancient Greek sculpture and the mythology of classical Greece in the fifth century B. C. guide. The best place to dance is outdoors, in nature. The united and interdependent aesthetic intention of the dancer and the audience's response to seeing natural dancing combine physical and psychological well-being. The ideal cultural context for natural dancing, an imagined "Arcadian" environment, Moller believes is reemerging in America in the first quarter of the twentieth century. When Raymond and Isadora Duncan travelled to Greece, they tried to carry out what Moller only wanted her students to imagine.

H'Doubler uses the word "dancing," the physical activity, in the title of her first book, *A Manual for Dancing*. Like her, the other authors also use "Dancing" as the title of the field in the same way "Dance" is used today. The following examples illustrate this point:

> This "book is a helpful guide to those interested in this particular approach to dancing." (MD, 1921:Preface)

> The title of Section One is "Teaching Interpretative Dancing as an Educational Activity." (MD, 1921:7)

> The art of dancing defined: "Dancing is self-expression through the medium of bodily movement; revealing of mental and emotional states, stimulated and regulated or both usually by music." (MD, 1921:7)

> "A student's response to music is still not dancing." (MD, 1921:11)

If one substitutes "dance" or "a dance" in each instance where H'Doubler uses "dancing," these ideas, in today's understanding, would more accurately convey H'Doubler's reference to the field or to the entity which dancers perform when dancing. She defines dancing in its broadest sense: "it includes posture, gesture, pantomime, symbolism expressed by the body in its various members or in its totality and self abandonment and recreative pleasure" (DPE, 1925:34). For H'Doubler, "dancing" means the study of dance in its personal and cultural context. Is her choice of the word "dancing" significant?

Perhaps H'Doubler uses "dancing" and not "dance" because she does not recognize a dance as an entity, separate from the dancer who is dancing it: "The dance lacks the element of permanence of form that can be touched up and reproduced in a copy. It remains only in the visual memory of the onlooker and the kinesthetic memory of the dancer" (DPE, 1925:183-184). In her books, she does not discuss rehearsals for the performances she stages. The students compose dances, in solos and in groups, but she focuses on the experiential process and the beneficial results the students gain during the creative development of the work, not the final performance of the dance. Like Isadora, the resulting dance remains secondary to the dancer's experience of dancing it. Her definition of a dance as a form of art reflects these values: Dance is an art form since "the chief characteristic of all art is self-expression and like all expressive arts it takes deep root in human experience, feelings, and emotion" (MD, 1921:7). H'Doubler values the emotional content which artists convey in their arts more than the works themselves.

While H'Doubler's books focus on the educational value of creative dance, her ideas reflect the radical utopian attitude toward the arts as a way to save the common people from living degrading and wasteful lives. Her value of the activity of dancing, not the art form of dance, reflects this ideal. Strongly influenced by Isadora Duncan and Mary Beegle, especially in the central role rhythm plays in most of her analysis of dancing, she transforms the ideas of her teachers and intellectual guides into a manifesto for the benefit of composing creative self-expressive dances: educational dancing, she claims, can permanently change the lives of students who study it.

The ideas and information in Elder's *Dance, A National Art* demonstrate that the development of early twentieth-century modern dance took place in many settings. Numerous artists shared a similar vision that natural dancing for non-professional people could enhance their lives and spirits. These dancers believe in the Greek ideal, the value of creative expression for their students, the integration of all the arts, and the educational richness that results from the experience of natural dancing.

Similar to the others I analyze here, Margaret Morris's theory of dance and dance education underscores the activity of dancing integrated with the other arts. She based her movement system on Raymond Duncan's Greek dance positions; her own innovations accentuate vigorous natural daily movements. She integrates improvisation and composition with her technique training and takes the creative process farther than the other dancer-writers when she requires her students to be responsible for all the production aspects of the performance. She trusts the creative ability of all her pupils; indeed, everyone would benefit from this process of arts education.

These seven dancer-writers espouse the same ideals for dancing: everyone is capable of dancing and should have the opportunity to create and dance their own dances; great music should accompany their dancing; the arts should remain integrated in the manner they were in classical Greece; movement should be natural, in harmony with dancers' own bodies, and with nature; if possible, dancing should take place outdoors where audience members watching will be inspired to begin dancing themselves. The dancing experience will elevate the lives of the dancers and lead them to seek more beauty in their lives. To publicize the beauty of this dancing experience these authors joined forces with photographers and publishers to illustrate and publish their ideas.

9
Books and Dance Books

The dancer-writers studied in this book wrote books to communicate their ideas to a wide audience at an opportune time in the history of dancing and of publishing. Increased literacy, more leisure time, and greater affluence contributed to a larger pool of potential readers than had previously existed (Lane, 1980:3, 7). The writing, publishing, and sale of books multiplied in the first thirty years of this century; in England twice as many new books were published in 1913 as in 1901. The number of books purchased almost doubled during this time also. Since books reflect the cultural milieu in which they are produced, a closer look at the designs and kinds of dance books published at this time reveals the cultural forces which influenced their authors.

Because of fierce competition among established and upstart publishing houses, publishers offered book buyers an unusual number of choices in variety, cost, and design of books. The choices ranged from soft-covered books, now called "paperbacks," to leather-bound series of the classics. Children's books, school books, and art books appeared among the many new categories from which book purchasers could choose after the turn of the century. Publishers added a new special feature: photographs and color plates supplemented the line drawings that frequently illustrated books in previous centuries. If a book contained photographs, especially "color plates," publishers highlighted this information on the title page to entice potential purchasers to buy the book. Most of the books about dancing that I have examined in this study contain numerous photographs, and three of them have "color plates." Before discussing the function of the photographs in these books about dancing, I will explain in detail the subjects of the dance books available during the early part of this century to place the books by our dancer-writers into a broader context of other dance books of the time.

In the early years of the twentieth century people interested in reading about dance could choose among a variety of books: dance manuals offered instructions in the latest ballroom dances, historical works provided information about dance from all over the world, biographical or autobiographical accounts told personal stories, and overviews of theater dancing surveyed contemporary dance activities. A look at the books which Beegle and Crawford and H'Doubler listed as references provides more detail about the available choices. Perhaps because of their university affiliations and the academic context in which they worked, these dancer-writers included bibliographies in their books; none of the other dance authors did (see Chapter 7).

Beegle and Crawford's book contains an extensive bibliography which takes up one fourth of the book, seventy-eight pages. Dance is one of their twenty-three topics (section XX pp.345-350). Beegle's dance list, thorough and impressive for its breadth and depth of dance subjects, gives an overview of the available dance books. Though contemporary dance scholars are familiar with many of those books, neither Beaumont's *Bibliography of Dancing* nor Magriel's book of the same name lists some of them. Beegle and Crawford selected books found in large American libraries: the New York or Boston public, the Library of Congress, or at Yale, Columbia, or Harvard. Of the eighty-four dance books Beegle lists, sixteen, or one-fifth, are treatises: old dance manuals with exact directions for executing a selection of dances, the primary sources for the study of dance. Some of these dance treatises contain theoretical principles of dance and notations of the dances current at the time when they were published.

Beegle arranges the books in chronological order from the earliest book, Arbeau's *Orchesographie* (1588), to three entries from 1915, including Louis Chalif's two-volume *The Text Book of Dancing*. The list includes twenty-four books in French, eleven in German, two books on Japanese dance, and three journal articles on specialized dance topics. The range of subject areas in dance encompasses a wide spectrum of dance subjects: treatises from 1588 to 1915; seventeen general dance history books, dating from 1701 to the Kinneys' 1914 *The Dance: Its Place in Art and Life*; twenty-three books on specialized areas or topics in dance history from 1620 to 1913; eleven entries on games and dance festival activities from 1901 to 1915; Guimard Duplain's poem, "Ou l'art de la danse-pantomime" (1783); Gulick's *The Healthful Art of Dancing* (1912); one book on the fine arts; and Dalcroze's *The Eurhythmics of Jaques-Dalcroze*. Beegle annotates the Dalcroze entry, "Almost the only available work in English on this subject" (Beegle and Crawford, 1916:349). Only eight other dance entries have brief annotations describing the value of their texts or illustrations. Beegle and Crawford's unusually comprehensive list of dance books shows the kinds of dance books to which Beegle and other dance scholars had access.

Beegle's student and colleague, Margaret H'Doubler, divided her eight-page bibliography into five sections: Philosophical Background, Music and Music Appreciation, Dancing and Dancers, Miscellaneous (in which she listed Beegle and Crawford's book), and Magazine Articles. Except for a few new entries, H'Doubler used the bibliography from her 1921 book in her 1925 book. She added three new books to the dance section in 1925, two on dance education and one on dance history, published between 1921 and 1925. All the other books published before 1916 in H'Doubler's list one finds in Beegle's. Most of the books on H'Doubler's "Dancers and Dancing" list, fourteen out of sixteen, were published during the twentieth century and include works on dance history, past and present, one art book, and Dalcroze's book on Eurhythmics. Of those on her list only Lily Grove's *Dancing* (1895) and Gaston Vuillier's *History of Dancing* (1896) were published in the nineteenth century. Unlike Beegle, H'Doubler included no treatises but chose contemporary dance books for her bibliography. Though all but Margaret Morris's book were published by 1921, H'Doubler lists none of the books written by the dancer-writers (except Beegle's) in the present study. Even the articles of Isadora Duncan, though not yet collected in one volume, were published in a variety of other forms. H'Doubler's choice of books represents her set of values and her academic preferences: she focuses on contemporary dance, on general history, and on music. Bibliographer Paul Magriel categorized the books analyzed in this study under the heading "The Art of Dancing."

The art and craft of book-making played a noteworthy part in the physical presentation of these books. The size, layout, and enticements of the books by H'Doubler, Morris, Moller, and Elder provide clues about the books' appeal. Moller's and Morris's books are large; Moller's book measures twelve by eight inches and Morris's twelve by nine inches. The title of the book and the author's name are printed in gold on the covers of both. The page layout of both books is similar: they utilize a lot of white space—one-third or more—on each page. (See Plate 18.) The outer and bottom margins in Moller's book measure two inches and in Morris's three inches. Approximately one-third of each book contains photographs. Morris's contains forty photographs and 92 pages of text. Moller's book includes forty-three photographs and 115 pages of text, of which forty-three display only the caption for the photograph opposite it, leaving 72 pages of actual text. Clearly the photographs in the dancer-writers' books illustrate and amplify their verbal message about dancing to their readers. Chapter 10 below presents a detailed analysis of the photographs.

The books by H'Doubler, Beegle and Crawford, and Elder are common size, six by nine inches, and they are less ornate, though they also contain several photographs. Elder's twenty-eight page book contains eight photographs, one-third of the book. H'Doubler's *The Dance and Its Place in Education* presents only five photographs and has extra-wide outer and bottom margins, while Beegle and Crawford's book is standard size, with one-inch margins and only sixteen photographs.

Although at the end of the twentieth century illustrating dance books with photographs has become standard practice, at the beginning of the century a large number of photographs in dance books was unusual. Though the process for reproducing excellent photographs using the halftone plate was developed in the 1880s, only after World War I did book publishers reproduce photographs inexpensively enough to include many photographs in books on a regular basis (Tebbel, 1975:668). Beaumont's *A Bibliography of Dancing* lists twenty-one dance books published between 1891 and 1924 that contained plates. The number of their photographs ranges from two to 73. Ethel Urlin's *Dancing, Ancient and Modern* (1911) includes 73 plates with six photographs among them. Because of their design and the photographs they contain, the books by the dancer-writers deserve our examination as aesthetic objects.

In addition to those by Moller, Elder, and Morris, three other dance books written during the first thirty years of this century contained numerous photographs: Arnold Genthe's photographic essay with 92 photographs, *The Book of the Dance* (1916) (reprinted in 1920 and then more widely circulated), to be discussed in Chapter 10 below, and two dance books with similar titles published in 1912 in the United States—*Dancing and Dancers of Today* (with 47 photographs), by Caroline and Charles H. Caffin, and *Modern Dancing and Dancers* (with forty-seven photographs, eight of these in color), by John Ernest Crawford Flitch. The books by the Caffins and Flitch, listed in bibliographies of Beegle and Crawford and H'Doubler, were ground-breaking in their introduction of photographs to illustrate the dance; the title pages of each book prominently announced this innovation. And like the works by Moller and Morris, these books were large, ten and one-half by eight and one-half inches. Gold letters boldly announced the titles and names of the authors on their covers (see Plates 23 and 32).

Both Flitch and the Caffins worked as art critics; in their dance books they claimed to write only about dancers whom they had actually seen. Of the many intriguing features of their books, three stand out: First, Flitch and the Caffins accurately assessed the revolutionary state of dance in 1912 and predicted the historical contributions of several of the leading dancers they described. Second, the books are strikingly similar in content and form. Third, and most intriguing, is the coincidentally large number of photographs in these books. Examination of the features of Flitch's book and then of the book by the Caffins helps us assess the reasons for these art critics' interest in dance and the place of their books in dance literature in the early twentieth century.

Flitch's book was first published in England in 1911 by Grant Richards

Limited and one year later in the United States by J. B. Lippincott. J. E. Crawford Flitch is listed in *Who Was Who in Literature, 1906-1934*, where he is described as translator of *Manet and the French Impressionists* by T. Duret, 1910; author of *Mediterranean Moods*, 1911; *The National Gallery*, 1912; *Modern Dancing and Dancers*, 1912; *A Little Journey in Spain; The Great War: Fourth Year*, 1918; and the translator from the Spanish of Unamuno's *Tragic Sense of Life*, 1921. Flitch, the landlord of Trout Inn, a public house and inn in Godstow, Oxford, was regarded as a remarkable amateur translator (Unamuno, 1972:xxv). (No birth and death dates for Flitch are listed in any available source, even in the Library of Congress listing of his works. All the available biographical sources were consulted: publishing houses were called, and the Librarian in the Laban Center, Goldsmiths College, University of London was consulted. This piece of information is absent even in the London Times Obituary Index. Flitch is not a pen name.) In his introduction to *Modern Dancing and Dancers*, Flitch refers to himself as a dance critic. Though most of Flitch's other books focus on literature and the visual arts, it is possible that, like other critics of the time, his newspaper assigned him to review dance performances, since no full-time dance critics were employed until around 1927. (During the first decades of this century in the United States, critics such as H. T. Parker and Carl Van Vechten, whose dance reviews have recently been collected and published, reviewed drama and music as well as dance performances). Flitch obviously became familiar enough with dance events and the performance criteria to review them. Beaumont, in his *A Bibliography of Dancing*, makes an exception to his rule of neutral reporting of a book's contents when he praises Flitch's book: "An admirably written and well illustrated book. The author has a wide knowledge of his subject, and his criticisms are invariably just and imbued with a real understanding of the ideals of the dance" (Beaumont, 1963:75).

Why did Flitch write his dance book? Flitch believed dance at that time was revolutionary, and he offered his views about the current rebirth of dance as an art in dance history. He predicts, "It is not unlikely that when the art historian of the future comes to treat of the artistic activity of the first decade of the twentieth century, he will remark as one of its most notable accomplishments a renaissance of the art of the Dance" (Flitch, 1912:9). Flitch explains how contemporary dancers vary considerably in their styles yet share the common aim of creating dances which meet the highest criteria of the principles of art.

In his book Flitch includes brief chapters on the origins of dance; the history of ballet; the development of the Russian Ballet; a survey of "eccentric" styles of dance, including Skirt, Serpentine, Oriental, and Spanish; and the revival of folk dancing. He gives equal consideration to ballet and natural (later called "modern") dance. Flitch calls the "natural" dance of Isadora Duncan "classical dancing." Judging from the contents of his book, the dance scene of the first decade of this century was rich, varied, and innovative: dances were performed by solo artists, and companies; they featured ballet and "natural" dancers; they derived from ritual, social, and "folk" forms; and they were based on traditional and novel choreographic methods.

In his discussion of the dancers, Flitch comments on major features of their performances. He praises their beauty and their dancing ability, both technical and dramatic. For instance, in his chapter on Isadora Duncan, he notes her choice of symphonic music as accompaniment, her use of "natural" movement so unlike ballet technique, her use of movements from Greek art, her body so unlike that of a traditional theater dancer, and her dance school for training children who give successful performances. Though he describes Duncan's technique as limited, he does not feel it detracts from the success of her dancing. The innovations of Duncan become the criteria to which Flitch compares other experimental artists such as Maud Allan and Ruth St. Denis.

In his description and analysis of Duncan's work, Flitch explains her theory of dance. In his exposition he borrows ideas and even phrases from the essays Duncan wrote and published in many of her dance programs. Though he does not actually cite his source, he credits her and quotes from her essay "The Great Source," written between 1904 and 1911 and used in her programs in England and France (Duncan, 1928:146).

Flitch shows great enthusiasm for Diaghilev's Russian Ballet and claims that this company has created a major change in the art of dance. He offers his remarkably accurate assessment only two years after Diaghilev's company first appeared in Paris, in 1909. After a brief history of ballet in Russia, he details the rigorous training which Russian dancers undergo. He then praises Diaghilev's ability to coordinate the choreography with the composition of the music, the design of the costumes, and the sets for the ballets. This type of collaboration, he notes, is uncommon for most other ballet companies he has seen recently. He then proclaims:

> The Russian ballet, which had been welcomed as the most modern manifestation of theatrical art, was not traditional but revolutionary. It was not the child of the official art of St. Petersburg but the outcast. Its leaders were dangerous innovators whom the intransigent conservatives had expelled as hastily as if they had been political agitators. . . . The truth

is that the excellence of the Imperial School of Ballet of which I have
spoken is an excellence of method and technique rather than of spirit and
conception. (Flitch, 1912:129)

In Flitch's contrast between the old tradition-bound Imperial School and
Diaghilev's ballet, he underscores the originality and freedom of Diaghilev's
ballet and recognizes its affinity to the new "natural" forms of dance.

Flitch summarizes and praises the ballets which he has seen the Russian
Ballet perform: *Le Pavillon d'Armide, Le Carnaval, Prince Igor, Les Sylphides, Le
Spectre de la Rose, Cleopatre,* and *Scheherazade.* These ballets, Flitch declares, are
outstanding because, "The ballet has been brought into relation with life"
(Flitch, 1912:131). He also praises the dancing of Vaslav Nijinsky, Tamara
Karsavina, Anna Pavlova, Mikail Mordkin, and Lydia Kyasht. To explain the
impact Diaghilev's company has had on ballet, Flitch quotes an unnamed
correspondent of the *London Times* who declared, "Alas! many pleasant illusions
have been shattered thereby, many idols have tumbled from their pedestals; we
have grown up terribly fast and lost the power of enjoying things that pleased
our callow fancies a year or two ago" (Flitch, 1912:173).

The placement of the photographs in Flitch's books can be confusing; they
often appear in chapters where he does not write anything about the dancer or
even the type of dance pictured. The photographs occur every two to nine pages.
Throughout Flitch's book in most cases the photographs are placed inside the
first and last pages of each signature. Some appear after the third or fourth page
or two pages from the end of a signature. Four pictures of Mikail Mordkin appear
in Flitch's book. One appears in a chapter where its relevance is questionable,
in Flitch's last chapter, "The Future of the Dance," where Flitch describes dance
used in a way similar to our contemporary aerobic dance. Because the same
photographs of famous dancers tend to be reprinted in recent dance books, the
unusual selection of pictures in Flitch's book of Ruth St. Denis, Maud Allan, and
Pavlova is refreshing (see Chapter 10 below and Plates 36–37).

An American publisher, Dodd, Mead, which earned a reputation in the early
part of this century for publishing current and even avant-garde American
literature at a time when other American publishers still reprinted the work of
established European authors, published the Caffins' book. In 1978 Da Capo
Press reprinted the Caffins' book. The catalogue description of the book by the
Caffins reads: "The 1912 book is still one of the best surveys of the origins and
development of dance. With chapters on American and Australian tribal dances,
the Greek synaesthetic ideal, medieval European pageants, and descriptions of

well-known and long forgotten founders of modern dance, it fills many lacunae in dance research." This catalogue announcement exaggerates the book's merits and misrepresents its contents: the chapters on American and Australian tribal dances, the Greek synaesthetic ideal, medieval European pageants are *not* in the Caffins' book but are the first chapters of Ethel Urlin's *Dancing: Ancient and Modern* (1911).

Like Flitch, Charles Caffin was British and he too was a professional art critic. Caffin (1854-1918) came to the United States from England in 1892. In 1897, he settled in New York and wrote art criticism for *Harper's Weekly*, the New York *Evening Post*, the New York *Sun, International Studio,* and the *New York American.* Between 1901 and 1917, he wrote seventeen popular and influential art books. Caffin's early training was in theater. He wrote his only other non-visual art book, *The Appreciation of Drama,* in 1908; it includes twelve plates and none are photographs. In the introduction to *Dancing and Dancers of Today*, Charles Caffin claims that his wife Caroline (1864-??) wrote an article, "The Camera and Isadora Duncan," which they quote in their chapter on Isadora Duncan. Charles Caffin himself wrote an article on Isadora Duncan, "Henri Matisse and Isadora Duncan" (*Camera Work* No. 25, 1909:17-20). There is no listing for Caroline Caffin's article in *Reader's Guide to Periodical Literature* or in the Index to *Camera Work,* though in 1914 she did write the book *Vaudeville* (New York, Kennerley, 1914) and an article, "Vaudeville Agent" in *Forum* in July, 1914 (50:103-109). Her book includes 49 plates of caricatures by Spanish artist Marius de Zayas. An exhibition of his work was displayed at Gallery 291 in 1908, and his drawings were frequently featured on the covers of *Camera Work* (see Plate 25). Caroline Caffin's motivation for writing her book may have been like that of her husband Charles, to disseminate a new art to a wider audience.

In the bibliography of her *Dance, A Creative Art Experience* (1940), H'Doubler confidently recommends the Caffins' *Dancing and Dancers of Today*: "This book, in addition to biographical chapters on the dance of Duncan, Maud Allen, Ruth St. Denis, Mordkin, Pavlova, and Grete Wiesenthal, contains historical material on the origin of ballet, court dances, and folk dancing pertinent to the dance of the time of the writing of the book" (H'Doubler, 1940:187). In her annotation H'Doubler accurately summarizes the information in the Caffins' book, noting its value in representing the current state of dance.

In their book, the Caffins place what they identify as "the dance revival" in the context of American culture. They claim: "Today, in America, we have awakened to the consciousness that dancing may be something more than a form of social amusement in ballrooms, or of gymnastic exercise on the stage.

We are taking a keen interest in the art of the Dance" (Caffin and Caffin, 1912:3). In one sentence, the Caffins describe the limited nature of theater dance in the late nineteenth century and its recent metamorphosis. They also place dance in a broader cultural context by pointing out that American audiences are maturing and becoming aware of the qualities and standards of fine art and its value in everyday life: "We regard the arts no longer as exotics, only to be enjoyed at rare moments of leisure, but as a necessity of civilised life" (Caffin and Caffin, 1912:7). In his book on the history of photography, written in 1904, Caffin had complained that Americans had no taste for the finer things in life. Eight years later, their changing taste in the new forms of theater dance convinced him to modify his opinion.

The Caffins' chapter on Isadora Duncan is quite similar to Flitch's. They survey the same topics and essentially come to the same conclusion. Their chapter includes more discussion of other arts than does Flitch's chapter. They too quote extensively from Duncan's writing, namely her 1909 essay "The Dance of the Future" (Duncan, 1928:55–59).

The Caffins' book contains chapters on the same topics which Flitch covers. They entitle their chapters by the name of the dancer, while Flitch uses the type of dance for his titles. Like Flitch, the Caffins discuss the Russian Ballet in three chapters. Their assessment of the Russian dancers' training agrees with Flitch's. The Caffins also applaud the collaboration among the musicians, set designers, costumers, and choreographer in what they call, in the captions of several photographs, the "Russian Dance-dramas." They praise the plots of the ballets:

> And truly no one can see these dance-dramas of the new Russian movement without realising that a new form has been imparted to this art. Here is realism not content with giving us the mere fact, but expressing the significance of the fact so forcefully that it is enhanced fifty-fold. No longer is it personal and peculiar to the individual, but universal and typical of the elemental forces from which it proceeds. (Caffin and Caffin, 1912:149-150)

The Caffins' praise for the plots of the Russian Dance-dramas agrees with Flitch in that "universal" and "elemental" forces certainly tell us about life. The Caffins laud each ballet as "a series of pictures for the painter, statues for the sculptor, stories for the romancer, psychology for the scientist and a Thing of Beauty for every eye" (Caffin and Caffin, 1912:155).

The Caffins base the praise they lavish on the Russian Dance-dramas of

Sheherazade and *Cleopatra* on the versions of these ballets that Gertrude Hoffmann mounted in the United States. Hoffmann became famous for imitating well-known dancers, such as Isadora Duncan, Ruth St. Denis, and Maud Allan (Cohen: 1977). The Caffins highly acclaim Hoffmann's Russian dancers:

> Their perfect technique and dramatic fire have so astonished us, that for the most part we have not had time to study the details of their art. Their innate sense of rhythm, which can correlate a seemingly unregulated rush and swirl of movement; the minutely studied psychology of the various gestures and poses; the artistic accord of technique and emotion—all these things, which every amateur of music studies at the opera as a matter of course, we have not yet learned to treat seriously in the Art of the Dance. (Caffin and Caffin, 1912:176)

The art of dance, assert the Caffins, has finally achieved what other modern arts have accomplished, since dancers now convey emotional expression and natural rhythmic force in their performances.

The Caffins explain that Gertrude Hoffmann went to Europe to study with the Diaghilev company for two years. They assume she reproduced complete versions of Diaghilev's original ballets being seen in Europe. Cyril Beaumont, in his annotation of the Caffins' book in A *Bibliography of the Dance Collection of Doris Niles and Serge Leslie,* credits their recognition of Hoffmann: "The part played by Gertrude Hoffmann in bringing Russian Ballet to these shores may be read with interest." (Beaumont also calls attention to the enjoyable photographic reproductions in their book.) Diaghilev's company did not tour North and South America until 1915-1916. Nonetheless, the Caffins' praise of the dancers' technique and the quality of the ballet plots was quite similar to Flitch's praise. The Caffins apparently did not know that Hoffmann's versions of the Russian Ballets were inauthentic reproductions. This lack of concern for authenticity gives clues to the limited depth and value of the Caffin book.

As in Flitch's book, the placement of the photographs in the books by the Caffins can be puzzling. Why are the photographs placed in chapters in which they do not illustrate the text? Are our expectations inappropriate for books with photographs at that time? The placement in the Caffins' book relates even less to the structure of the page signatures than in Flitch's book. In their chapter on Isadora Duncan, for instance, a portrait of Duncan by Edward Steichen appears on the second page. On the tenth page of the chapter is a photograph of Russian dancers Lydia Popoukowa and Mikail Mordkin by Clarence White, and on the fifteenth page appears a picture of Ruth St. Denis by Otto Sarnoy. The Caffins include eight pictures of Mikail Mordkin and place them in chapters in which they do not relate such as in the chapters on Isadora Duncan and Eccentric Dancing. The dancers in the group photos entitled "Russian Dancers" do not appear to be highly trained; these photos also appear in unrelated chapters (see Plates 28, 29, 30). How does one explain the selection of these photographs and their unusual placement in these books by the Caffins and Flitch?

The primary stated purpose of Flitch and the Caffins in writing their books is to analyze and record the revolutionary changes in dance in the first decade of the twentieth century. They claim to describe only dances and dancers which they witnessed, and they compare the quality of the dance innovations with the gymnastic, mechanical, and expressionless dance which they had seen until then. Their books survey almost the same dancers, except that Flitch does not mention Rita Sacchetto and only briefly mentions Grete Wiesenthal, whereas the Caffins devote separate short chapters to these artists. They agree about the significance of each dancer in the current artistic "revival" of dance. By 1912 Isadora Duncan, Maud Allan, Anna Pavlova, and Adeline Genee reached only the middle of their careers while Mikail Mordkin and Ruth St. Denis had just begun theirs. Yet from the vantage point of only the first decade, the Caffins and Flitch perceptively assess how each dancer contributed to dance in the twentieth century. In retrospect, the ability of the authors to predict the significance of the artists who created the revival of dance is remarkable.

Flitch's reputation as a dance critic seems to be more established than that of the Caffins though neither Charles Caffin nor J.E. Crawford Flitch is listed as a dance critic in any recent dance encyclopedia or dictionary (see end of References for those works consulted). No articles about dance by these "dance critics" can be found in any guide to periodical literature. A careful search of the many newspapers of the time might yield some articles on dance by the Caffins and Flitch, but that undertaking is beyond the scope of this book. Beaumont does not list the Caffins' book in his bibliography of dance books, and neither does the biographer who wrote about Charles Caffin in the *Dictionary of American Biography* (1929). Magriel, in his bibliography of dance books, categorizes the Caffins' book under "Biography and Memoirs" and Flitch's under "Modern History." Caffin was highly regarded in art circles for contributing to the appreciation of contemporary art, especially art photography. From the evidence presented here, however, his authority on dance should be questioned.

What shall we make of the great similarities of the books of the Caffins and Flitch even though they differ when the Caffins base their praise of the Russian

Ballet on the renditions of a famous imitator? The parallels between their books are too great to ignore. As critics the authors saw many of the same performers, especially the most widely acclaimed dancers who toured New York and London. And as critics, they analyze the key features of any dance performance: the dancer's technique, the dancer's beauty, the dramatic impact of the dancing, the originality of the choreography, and the relationship between the dance and the music, the costumes, and the sets.

Despite their explicit content and their accurate assessment of the state of dance, clarification of the nature of these books will contribute to understanding their similarities and their limitations. At first they appear to fit into the genre of dance books written to explain and popularize an activity not widely understood by large numbers of people. The titles of the books focus on dance activity which is immediate and contemporary. Dance critics John Martin in the 1930s, in his *America Dancing* (1936), and John Percival in the 1970s, in his *Experimental Dance* (1971), wrote just such books.

The books of the Caffins and Flitch contain such extensive praise for the dancers and dancing that they may fit another category. The books read like a series of carefully crafted positive press releases, known in the trade as "puffs." A puff is a pseudo-review written to give favorable publicity to the dancer or artist, and often quotes an artist's own words, such as the ones the Caffins and Flitch used in their praise of Isadora Duncan. For other dancers about whom they write, they frequently quote available books, such as Maud Allan's autobiography and other contemporary dance critics. They fill their chapters with information about the other arts, especially painting and sculpture. Writing puffs was a common theatrical practice in Europe and America during the eighteenth and nineteenth centuries. Theater managers or their agents offered tickets, refreshments, and private rooms in the theater to newspaper owners, their families, and critics in exchange for favorable reviews in their papers. The author of a puff habitually heaped lavish praise on the artists in question (Miller, 1981:5). Since dance is a theater art, and since the critics who reviewed theatrical performances covered the other performing arts, it follows that they wrote puffs for performances of dance companies just as they wrote them for theater performances. Though a puff functions in a newspaper or on a billboard to bring audiences into performances, a collection of them in a book cannot possibly serve that purpose. What, then, was the purpose of these books? This question may be answered when we clarify their extensive use of photographs.

The number of photographs—forty-seven—in the books by the Caffins and

Flitch is unusual for dance books of the early twentieth century, which were usually illustrated with drawings. (The books by Moller and Morris were published after World War I.) Flitch reproduces none of the photographs found in the Caffin volume. A closer look at the photographic credits offers pertinent information to evaluate the nature of these books. Clarence White of New York took twenty-seven of the forty-seven photographs in the Caffin book. White photographed all of the "Russian Dancers" including five of the eight photographs of Mikail Mordkin. Clarence White, a well-known pictorialist photographer, became a founding member of the Photo-Secessionist Movement, a revolutionary group of photographers led by Alfred Stieglitz from his New York gallery "291." Caffin published a seminal article, "Rumpus in the Hen-House," in *Camera Work*, no. 22, 1908, describing Stieglitz's challenge to the artistic status quo. Along with Stieglitz, White is a significant enough pictorialist to warrant a profile to be written about him in a recent history of photography (Rosenblum, 1989:337-338). The goal of the Photo-Secessionists was to have photography recognized as an art form (Larkin, 1960:358-360). These photographers modeled their work on the art of Whistler, Corot, Millet, and the Barbizon School. The art photographers became known as pictorialists. Among their favorite subjects were portraits of nudes, bucolic landscapes, and dancers. In contrast, non-pictorial photographers used the camera to take pictures of reality from scenes of wars and poverty to celebrations of aboriginal peoples around the world.

As an art critic, Charles Caffin became well known for his support and defense of the Photo-Secessionists, and he wrote regularly for the highly regarded quarterly magazine *Camera Work* (1903-1917), founded, edited, and published by Stieglitz. Indeed, Caffin wrote one or more articles in each issue. In 1903, and again in 1908, Caffin wrote separate articles about Clarence White. In 1903, 1909, and 1910 Caffin wrote articles about Edward Steichen, another famous photographer of this group (more widely known to dance scholars for his photographs of Isadora Duncan in Greece) who has one photograph in the Caffin book. Caffin may well have been motivated to publish his dance book to publicize and distribute dance photographs, especially those of White. When looking through the Caffin book we get the impression that they wrote chapters about dancers of whom they had photographs; that might account for an entire chapter on Rita Sacchetto, whose name cannot be found in any other dance history book of the time (see Plate 31).

Flitch, also an art critic, may have been a supporter of the British art photographers. Their group in England was called The Linked Ring. The

English recognized art photography before the art establishment in America did. Early in his career, Stieglitz found encouragement to pursue his art photography there, and later he published the work of many British photographers in his *Camera Work*. Stieglitz belonged to The Linked Ring, as well as to his own group. Some of the photographers of the dancers in Flitch's book were probably part of that movement since several of the photographs are in the romantic portrait style popular among the pictorialists. Many of the photo credits in his book are listed only by photographic studio. The few individual photographers whose names he gives are not listed in any history of photography, but some of the studios listed became known for taking dance photographs. Thus, my observation about Flitch's support of pictorial photography remains an informed conjecture. Photograph credits in Flitch's book are as follows: W. and D. Downey; Ellis and Walery; Central Illustrations; Dover Street Studios, Ltd.; Foulsham and Banfield, Ltd.; Gershe; Bert, Paris; Bassano, Ltd.; and Campbell Grey. Eleven of the plates are paintings, or drawings of famous dancers. Photographs in the Caffin book are almost all credited to Photo-Successionists: White, N.Y.; Notman, Boston; Edward J. Steichen; Otto Sarnoy; Franz Grairer, Munich; Pieter Mijer; and Jessie Tarbox Beals who photographed a dance composed by Mary Beegle (see Plate 27).

In the early twentieth century, authors who wrote about dance often acted as advocates for their developing art, thus, the scholarly criterion of objectivity did not guide their highly selective writing. The Caffins and Flitch not only recorded their views on dance at that time, but their books also publicized another emerging art; thus, these authors appear to have as a significant secondary purpose the distribution of the work of contemporary art photographers.

How do the books by our dancer-writers relate to the two books by the art critics? The titles of the books help answer this question. The dancer-writers focus primarily on dancing, whereas in their books, the Caffins and Flitch focus on dancing *and* dancers; though the visions of the dancer-writers and the art critics overlap, they also differ. The art critics focus on individually acclaimed dancers and photographs of them to make their points. The dancer-writers concentrate on the newly developing artistic form of dancing, while the Caffins and Flitch also include other forms of dancing they saw on theater stages of the day. All the writers verify the impact and importance of Isadora Duncan as the major innovator. And all the writers use the newly developing medium of photography to illustrate, enhance, and reinforce their words. The dancer-writers welcomed innovation in other arts as well as in their own. What these photographs tell us about the dancing, the dancers, the photographers, and the techniques of both arts is the subject of the next chapter.

10
Photography and Dance Photographs

In the early part of the twentieth century, the Photo-Secessionists' struggle for recognition of photography as an art occurred as part of a complete revolution in the visual arts in America and Europe. The revolt against the academic standards of art arose not just among photographers, but among artists who worked in many techniques, media, and formats. The artists argued about the purpose of art: should it represent reality or beauty? Advocates of beauty valued "art for art's sake," whereas the realists, with the radical utopians among them, often saw art as a means to supply graphic information to communities, persuade people to take action, enrich their private lives, and brighten the lives of their viewers. The artists in each ideological camp not only differed in the techniques they used but disagreed about the subject matter they chose to record. Some art photographers stressed beauty, such as the Photo-Secessionists, and some stressed utility. The utilitarians used their photographs to provide facts, truth, and actuality, often for newspaper and documentary reporting. An intermediate group combined the two extremes. When the dancer-writers used the pictorial style of photography in their books they took advantage of both the beauty and utilitarian features of this sister art.

Art photographers strove against two interrelated stigmas in their campaign to gain recognition for photography as an art. In 1880 George Eastman invented and successfully marketed roll film. Within ten years he popularized the Kodak Brownie camera which sold for one dollar; fifteen cents paid for replacement film. This technological breakthrough enabled anyone to be a photographer. People no longer considered the professional photographer essential to document important events in their lives. This combination of technology and marketing threatened the profession itself. The people who controlled the established art world regarded photography as a mere past-time for amateurs and not an artistic endeavor. The camera, a mechanical device, created the other perceived disadvantage. Since art experts valued "art" for its originality and its hand-made qualities, photographs, according to these criteria, did not qualify as authentic art.

Leaders among the Photo-Secessionists, such as Alfred Stieglitz and Clarence White, worked to overcome the negative stigmas assigned to the artistic value of photography by the public and the art world. The pictorialists doctored the negatives of their photographs to achieve art-like qualities in the final pictures.

The most recognizable characteristic of a pictorial photograph is its fuzzy or blurry and softened background. Pictorialists sought to evoke an emotional response in the viewer by using light, shade, breadth, concentration of focus, and strength of subject matter to achieve painterly qualities. They even softened the details and sharp lines of the main subject to highlight values, textures, and character, making a photograph imitate a painting. Unfortunately, the painting style they imitated—that of Whistler, Corot, Millet, and the Barbizon School—embodied the upper-class taste for sentimentality where paintings often portrayed superficial aspects of life, such as gaiety, frivolity, sorrow, and anger in a manner that appealed to people of means and wealth.

People who purchased art also invested in books both for their content and for their aesthetic qualities. Because of the unprecedented growth in methods of photomechanical replication between 1880 and World War I, inexpensive ways of reproducing photographs enabled publishers to use them in their books especially after World War I. Publishers, explains photography historian Weston J. Naef, preferred certain kinds of photographs in their books: the photographs should communicate truthfulness or the illusion of truth if they were "to be an essential ingredient of a successful photographically illustrated book" (Goldschmidt, 1980:36). Evidently, the publishers of the books written by the dancer-writers believed that their photographs satisfied this criterion.

A book with photographs cost more than one without them. Collectors regarded these unusual books as art objects in their own right. Their readership, therefore, was limited to upper-middle and upper-class book purchasers. Naef describes the special process of constructing a book which included photographs:

> The most common design was to place a single photograph mounted on a separate single leaf facing a text page. Photographically illustrated books were not, therefore, customarily constructed out of sheets of paper folded and sewn, but rather were unfolded leaves glued at the spine with rubber-like gutta-percha as the adhesive. (Goldschmidt, 1980:52)

The bindings of books constructed in this manner, Naef points out, deteriorated easily and fell apart more quickly than books with sewn bindings. My copies of the books with many photographs examined in this study have glued bindings and have deteriorated just as Naef predicted.

In the introduction to his recent book, *Dance and Photography* (1987), photography authority William A. Ewing places dance photography of this period into its historical context. In the 1860s, dancers were favorite subjects for photographic *carte-de-visite* size cards (the size of a business card, six by nine centimeters) which wealthy and middle-class admirers collected. When this fad waned and collecting post-card sized photographs took its place, the mechanical and chemical developments of photography had not progressed sufficiently to prevent artificially-posed studio portraits from continuing to be taken even during the first third of the twentieth century. Early twentieth-century dance-photographers, Ewing explains, followed the nineteenth-century tradition of picturing dancers in a manner similar to the idealized lithographs of romantic ballerinas. This type of lithograph and photograph created an image of the dancer as idol and did not convey the power and vitality of her dancing. Ewing identifies how photography can serve dance: to make a record and document of the dance or dancer, to invent special effects in the photograph, to make the dancer into an icon or idol, to show a tour de force of the dancer's dancing, or to create a collaborative relationship that achieves the goals of both the photographer and dancer. Some of these purposes serve the dancer and the dancing—showing arrested motion which typifies the dance's essence or the dancer's unique capability—some serve the photographer and the photograph—displaying artistic effects, moods, and techniques—while some serve both.

A systematic analysis of the photographs in the books I have studied here will clarify how the pictorial medium functioned to communicate about dancing. To compare the photographs I will examine the following features: background, camera angle, distance from the subject, location, and then the number of dancers, posed or in motion, their costumes, and the shape of their postures and gestures. An overview of the photographs in each book begins this analysis.

In the book of Isadora Duncan's writings, Sheldon Cheney included twenty-four drawings (see examples in Plates 69 and 70) and only nine photographs. Authors of dance history books frequently reproduce almost all of these photographs. Four are by Edward Steichen and five by Arnold Genthe; both these photographers started their careers in the Photo-Secessionist group of American pictorial photographers. The photographs by Steichen and Genthe serve the photographer as art photographer; in only two do viewers get a glimpse of Isadora dancing. The photographers did not intend to show her dancing. They admired her accomplishments in revolutionizing the art of dancing and simply wanted to capture her essence in pictorial terms and immortalize her in their art, not hers.

Of the sixteen photographs in Beegle and Crawford's book, three show open-

air theaters, three picture individuals, and the rest capture large groups ranging
from five to seventeen dancers performing in pageants. The authors distribute
the photographs throughout the book and do not just place them in the chapters
on dance. They include two photographs of dancers not performing in pageants
by professional photographers, Ira Hill of a Morgan dancer and Arnold Genthe
of the Florence Fleming Noyes dance group. (Arnold Genthe includes both
these dance groups in his book.) The photographs in Beegle and Crawford's
book coordinate with the purpose of their book: the illustrations provide
instruction and do not intend to be art. Some of them convey motion and show
the type of dancing Beegle recommends (see Plates 1-6).

Helen Moller herself took many of the forty-three photographs in her book.
She also gives credit to the professionals who took some of them—Moody,
Maurice Goldberg, Charles Albin, Underwood and Underwood, and Genthe—
though she did not place the credits with the photographs themselves. Frequently she frames the photographs in circles, arches, or rectangles, a device the
Photo-Secessionists used to make their work appear like paintings. Two pictures
show a Greek statue and Roman copy of it, thirteen show individuals, and the
rest picture groups of three to ten dancers. Moller's photographs serve several
related pedagogical purposes. Since she took many of the photographs herself
and placed them on almost every other page, she integrated them into her book,
making the book itself an art object. Some of her photographs imitate pictures
of well-known pictorial art photographs and relate only indirectly to the
dancing she espouses. The majority of the photographs document her techniques, the style and variety of her costumes, her attitude toward the body, and
the relationship of her dancing to classical Greek ideals (see Plates 12-17).

The photographs in Eleanor Elder's little book contain four group shots of
seven to fourteen men or men and women performing a natural dance in India,
and four single shots of Raymond Duncan's six Greek positions; two of these
photographs show two positions. The two kinds of photographs in Elder's book
serve different purposes. The photographs of the Greek positions of Duncan
supplement line drawings and give human form to Elder's instructions. The
photographs of the dancers performing natural dances demonstrate the renaissance in dancing among people of all walks of life. None of the photographs
show any motion; they are decidedly static (see Plates 18-23).

In The *Dance and Its Place in Education* Margaret H'Doubler includes only five
photographs taken by George Bell of Milwaukee; all in the pictorial style, with
fuzzy, filmy, and misty backgrounds outdoors in highly romanticized nature.
One pictures dancers indoors against a dark background. Only one shows a

single dancer, while the others have two, four, and five dancers. Since H'Doubler de-emphasizes dance performance, these photographs mainly set the scene for the quality of the dance experience she espouses: uplifting, serene, romantic, and part of nature (see Plates 7-11).

In contrast to the other books in this study, the placement of photographs in Margaret Morris's book is unusual. She lists her photographer as the second author of her book. She collects the forty photographs, all taken outdoors by Fred Daniels, as the first section of her book and then refers to them in her text. The captions of the photographs range from simple titles of the dances, from which the pictured movement comes, to comments about the goals of her movement technique and about the line, shape, or group design illustrated in the pictures. Some of the photographs show her students resting, recreating, eating watermelon, and taking class; thus, all do not deepen a reader's understanding of Morris's dance goals, though they do illustrate the ambience of her summer school sessions. The photographs help sell her way of dancing to her readers, since they show something for everyone, from resting, eating, and swimming to taking class and performing in several natural settings.

In his photographs Steichen poses Isadora Duncan outside in the Parthenon in Greece. He shot all but one from a great distance; the one which is closer, like most of the photographs in all the books, pictures Isadora's entire body. In this one she faces the camera directly, an unusual gaze for these photographs, while in the others Isadora gazes up or out, not directly into the camera. For the most part, the indirect gaze and camera angle reflect the pattern which emerged throughout the photographs in the books of our dancer-writers. Genthe's two famous portraits of Isadora look like painted portraits with dark backgrounds and softened details. In his others Isadora also poses, indoors with dark backgrounds: seated in profile and reclining in one picture and reaching upward with both arms in two others. In only one of Genthe's portraits does Isadora directly face the camera.

Five of the sixteen photographs in Crawford and Beegle's book show the dancers in motion, outdoors: with the ocean, the woods, or a field as uniformly fuzzy backgrounds. In all the photographs they capture the entire body; the distance from which they are taken encompasses large groups of dancers spread entirely across a twenty-five foot grassy stage space.

The indoor photographs in Moller's book have plain white wall or dark backgrounds; while the outdoor shots show field, beach, or woods. These outdoor settings represent the idealized version of nature about which Moller writes. Of all the photographs, only three picture the dancer gazing directly into the camera; in the others the dancers gaze up, back, down, or sideways in profile. The camera angle is frontal, and the distance in these shots is closer than in the other books. The dancers' bodies take up most of the photograph.

The group shots in Elder's book take place outside on a lawn with a few trees in the background, while the individual shots show an indoor dark background. These photographs of individuals picture the total body in profile. Most of the people dancing in the group photographs are also in profile, and only the central figures in two look directly into the camera. These outdoor pictures do not have fuzzy backgrounds.

Thirteen of the Fred Daniels' photographs picture a single dancer; most show Margaret Morris in her own dances. The group photographs picture from three to fifteen dancers. Almost all the photographs are posed. Eight show Morris's signature position, which exaggerates backwards the skipping pose seen in photographs in the other books by dancer-writers, where the dancer lifts one bent leg very high forward and spreads her uplifted arms which reach front and back with the torso rotated away from the bent forward leg (see plates 19, 20, 23). By 1926 Morris further developed the natural dance techniques, shown in the other dancer-writers' books, into more virtuosic and acrobatic positions and movements. This development parallels the development of faster film for which the dancers do not have to hold still for so long.

Isadora Duncan wears a long-sleeved flowing Greek cloak in all but one of Steichen's pictures; she wears her sleeveless Greek tunic in the closer shot. Except for the dancers in Margaret Morris's book, all the "natural" dancers in the photographs in the other books wear the same style Greek tunic, tied at the waist or tied higher to create a bodice. Only the length of the skirt and occasionally the color varies. In Genthe's photographs Isadora wears her longsleeved Greek tunic or a Greek wrap which she drapes over one shoulder.

In the photographs in Beegle and Crawford's book the dancers all wear sleeveless Greek tunics, and their arm gestures are often uplifted and spread wide in a movement similar to a frequently reproduced one of Isadora Duncan. The dancers gaze out, away, down, or at each other. Except for the Noyes photograph, the groupings are balanced yet asymmetrical (see Plate 43).

Five of the pictures in Moller's photographs show the upper half of the naked body—portraits—with dark background swallowing up the lower half of the body. The dancers in three other photographs are also naked; two of these are of children. (On 28 February 1918 Helen Moller appeared in court to answer a complaint of the Society for Prevention of Cruelty to Children. One of her students performed a pantomime and the judge dismissed the case.) The clothed dancers wear long and short Greek tunics or drapes wrapped in a manner similar to Greek sculpture. Only two of the photographs, taken on the beach, show dancers in motion. Otherwise the dancers pose with one foot forward of the other with the knee of that forward leg bent slightly or raised in a skipping position. Like the uplifted and far-spread arms in many of the photographs, this skipping position is also found throughout the photographs of natural dancers in all the books.

As in the pictures of the other books, the dancers in Elder's photographs wear Greek tunics which reach to the men's knees and the women's mid-calf. Raymond's Greek positions are shot from a closer distance than the outdoor ones; these indoor distances are similar to those of the photographs in the books by Moller and Beegle and Crawford.

In the photographs in H'Doubler's book two of the group photographs capture the dancers in motion in their flowing Greek tunics. As before, the distance from the camera of the indoor photograph is close enough to show the entire bodies of the dancers and little else. The distance of the outdoor shots captures the trees and water in the background with the dancers gazing up or out. One profile shot combines the upward reaching and far-spread arms of Isadora Duncan and the lifted bent knee of Hellen Moller's dancers.

Margaret Morris's dancers wear cotton bathing suits with short skirts sewn on below the waist. She and some of her adult dancers wear other costumes reminiscent of children's book illustrations of that day. Her costumes allow for the greater freedom needed to execute the virtuosic dancing she taught.

Most of the photographs in the books of the dancer-writers differ from those in the books by the Caffins and Flitch. Whereas photographs used by the art critics feature the dancers-as-idols, the dancer-writers primarily show positions of the new techniques which the natural dancers study; they highlight the dancing. The art critics chose posed publicity shots; the one exception in the Caffin book, a photograph of Mary Beegle's dancers, shows them dancing in an outdoor pageant. The natural outdoor background in many of the photographs in the dancer-writers' books conveys the healthy ambience they associate with their new form of dancing. Both kinds of photographs capture the limited positions which the dancers can hold while the photograph is being taken, though this changed as film and cameras improved.

The Book of the Dance (1916) by Arnold Genthe presents a goldmine of visual information about dancers of this time, especially in relation to the other dance books discussed here. Rosenblum in her *A World History of Photography* praises Genthe's work which he began as a photographer in the Photo-Secessionist

California Camera Club. Genthe's photographs, "though seen through the haze of a romanticizing vision, have a refreshing spontaneity that distinguishes them from more statically posed rural genre images" (Rosenblum, 1984:323). His 92 pictorial-style photographs provide a cross-check for our analysis of the preceding photographs.

In his introduction to Genthe's book, art critic Shaemas O'Sheel praises Genthe for his vision and imagination and explains why Genthe is uniquely qualified to produce this book: "To vast resources of knowledge and superior intellect, Dr. Genthe adds that keen sensitiveness and unquenchable enthusiasm which enable him to approach and pursue his problem with rare subtlety and devotion" (Genthe, 1916:xvi). Ewing comments on Genthe's background. German-born Genthe earned his Ph.D. in classics and modern languages, and then became an expert in travel, music, and the dance. In the early years of this century, Genthe's partnership with Isadora, Ewing claims, matches Baron Adolf de Meyer's partnership with Nijinsky for its rich collaborative insight. "Photography had come of age and its practitioners were ready to undertake a fruitful partnership with the revitalized world of dance" (Ewing, 1987:20).

In his Foreword, Genthe explains why he published this book:

> I merely wanted to show some of the phases of modern dance tendencies that could be recorded in a pictorially interesting manner. This, therefore, is meant to be just a picture book, permanently recording something of the fugitive charm of rhythmic motion, significant gesture and brilliant color which the dance has once more brought into our lives. (Genthe, 1916:5)

He goes on to apologize for not photographing the ballroom dancers of the day. The dismal black suits which the men must wear, he explains, prevented him from including them. He extends his gratitude to the dancers who let him photograph them and made it possible for him "to obtain pictures expressing something of the grace and fluency of dance motion" (Genthe, 1916:5).

Genthe's book offers a large sample of the "natural" dancers active during this time. His photographs represent five schools of natural dance: those of Duncan, St. Denis, Morgan, Noyes, and Biyar. He gives a section each to soloists Maud Allan, Lillian Emerson (a child), Loie Fuller, and Lady Constance Stewart Richardson (see Plate 48).

In 1913 Lady Constance Stewart Richardson published *Dancing, Beauty, and Games* (London: Arthur L. Humphreys) in which she includes several photographs: three of her children by Andrew Patterson of Inverness, three of Isadora Duncan, Adeline Genee, and Madam Karsavina by the Dover Street Studios, and two of herself photographed by the (Clarence) White Studios, entitled "Barefooted Dancing after the Greek Style" (see Plate 49, 50). She places these five in her short chapter on "Dancing," pages 55-62. Her chapter on Swimming contains two stunning photographs, uncredited, of two high dives, the "English Position" and the "Swedish Swallow Dive"; they capture the diver in flight from a great distance.

Except for Ruth St. Denis, these natural dancers all wear a Greek tunic of some kind. Genthe also pictures Spanish Dancers, Classical Dancers (all naked), Anna Pavlova (barefoot in two different Greek tunics), and a group he calls Eclectic Dancers. This last group of photographs includes dancers in Persian, Hawaiian, Egyptian, Javanese (bare breasted) and Ballroom costumes. He includes six of the photographs in color, and shows thirty-eight women and two photographs of one man, William Bayne. At the end of the book he lists the names of the dancers with pages to locate them. He selects seven photographs of Ruth St Denis, the most Genthe included of one dancer; others number three, two, or one.

Genthe displays his photographic signature in these pictures. Most (thirty-eight), show the dancer in profile; fewer (eighteen) in partial profile. Only seventeen picture the dancer directly from the front, though only six dancers gaze directly into the camera. Other dancers pose in a seated position or he photographs them from the back, with the dancer looking over her shoulder. He only chose two outdoor shots and these contain fuzzy backgrounds. He shot the twelve classical dancers, all naked, in natural dance positions and he does not list these dancers' names at the end of the book. At least seventeen of Genthe's photographs capture the dancer in motion with the skirts of their costumes suspended in the air. His photographs show the dancers he saw during this time through the lens of a brilliant photographer, but over eighty percent of them do not show much more about the dancing than the poses the dancers could hold. In contrast, his pictures of Pavlova are remarkable because he took the first photographs of her in free movement (Ewing, 1987:23).

At the end of his introduction to Genthe's book O'Sheel comments on the partnership between the arts of photography and dance:

> Pictorial art, which has the privilege and duty of ministering to the other arts, has done but ill heretofore in behalf of the dance. There have been many delicate sketches made and some really fine photographs, but these

have not been widely available, and the best books on the dance have been calamitously illustrated. Now at last this deficiency on the pictorial side has been supplied. The latest of the arts, photography, has been used by one of its greatest masters to give the world a definite, coherent, illuminating record of the modern art of the dance. (Genthe, 1916:xv-xvi)

O'Sheel's comments echo Ewing's. The success of this partnership depends on which partner's goals remain in focus. Photographers of any style—art, portrait, or realist—strive to make masterful photographs. Capturing the magic of dancing and the essence of the dancers, Ewing claims, has challenged photographers since they began taking photographs in the 1830s. Though by photographic standards experts consider some of the pictures in the books in this study masterpieces, from the dancer's side of the partnership the photographs record more about the dancers' appearances, costumes, and characteristic poses than they reveal about the dancing which most of the dancer-writers wanted to explain (see Plates 40-48).

In many photographs in the books under consideration, a characteristic pose appears repeatedly among the natural dancers. The dancer reaches her widespread arms high over her head, while lifting the knee of one bent leg in a skipping position. Variations of this include the torso bent back, the bent leg very high, and at times the dancer's torso twists so she looks over her shoulder. Can we know if this pose or movement represents an integral part of their dancing or just a signature pose for the camera? A look at two more books published during the time helps answer this question.

Several books show drawings and photographs of similar techniques: the Dalcroze Eurhythmics system, Delsarte exercises (adapted by one of his many students), and the technique of Isadora Duncan. In 1925, Jo Pennington published *The Importance of Being Rhythmic: A Study of the Principles of Dalcroze Eurhythmics Applied to General Education and to the Arts of Music, Dancing, and Acting, Based on and Adapted from "Rhythm, Music, and Education," by Emile Jaques-Dalcroze*. Pennington wrote three of the seven chapters and published translations of essays from Dalcroze's book. Of interest here are the drawings and photographs. One of the drawings illustrating crescendo is quite similar to H'Doubler's drawings for her "unfolding and folding" technique (see Plates 81, 82, 83, 84). The drawings in H'Doubler's books, and the drawings and photographs in Pennington's book closely resemble exercises in Irma Duncan's thirty-five page *The Technique of Isadora Duncan* (1937), with photographs by

Hans V. Briesen, posed by Isadora, Irma, and the Duncan pupils (see Plate 86). Though Irma Duncan published her book in the 1930s, she taught the techniques, recorded in the book, she claims, in Isadora Duncan's schools in Berlin and Russia. Because she intends to preserve Isadora Duncan's legacy, the twelve introductory lessons included in the book probably replicate those Isadora Duncan taught and danced in her repertoire. Since H'Doubler's drawings, Pennington's drawings and photographs, and Irma Duncan's photographs all record techniques, they can more easily be compared to each other than to movements in dances represented in photographs. The signature movements which appear in many of the photographs in the books of this time closely resemble the photographs in the technique sections of books. We can conclude that even though most of the photographs in the books by the dancer-writers satisfy the photographic side of the partnership more than the dance side, they do reveal a shared aesthetic and a common vocabulary of movement.

Is there a relationship among the Dalcroze techniques, the Delsartian exercises, Isadora Duncan's techniques, and the technique systems the other dancer-writers present in their teaching and in their books? Yes. They relate closely to each other, interpreting and varying "natural" movements: walking, running, skipping, hopping, and turning. Experts taught both the Delsarte and Dalcroze systems in schools as part of physical education or "physical culture" as it was called. From where did Dalcroze derive his techniques? Delsarte taught in Paris where Dalcroze went in 1883 to study acting and music. Dalcroze attended sessions taught by Delsarte. He also watched the children's classes of Isadora Duncan and had hoped to work together with her on a project though it never came to fruition. As a young man, he studied Swedish gymnastics when exponents brought the system to Switzerland.

In America Isadora and Raymond Duncan studied the Delsartian system before they became professional dancers and teachers, adapting it to their needs and combining it with their study of Greek movements. Midwestern dance teacher Leslie Clendenen's book, reprinted repeatedly between 1903 and 1919, includes chapters on each system. The drawings of the six Greek positions in his book replicate exactly the photographs of Raymond Duncan's six Greek positions in Eleanor Elder's book. Clendenen's written section on "Greek Dancing and Expression," pp. 46-52, also replicates most of the ideas in Elder's essay though he does not quote her. His chapter on "Esthetic and Rhythmic Dancing" combines the Dalcroze exercises with Delsartian ones presented in Eleanor Georgen's *The Delsarte System of Physical Culture* (1893). The Delsarte book represents just one of many published by Delsarte's students or their students in the United States. Pictures of "Tanagra Figures" in Irma Duncan's book (p.21) are similar to "Interpretative Posings" in Clendenen's book (p. 67) and "Oppositions" in Georgen's book (pp. 59-72) (see Plates 54, 55, 56, 58, 60). Thus even the posed photographs of the dancing in the books of the dancer-writers, through the lens of the camera, offer brief moments of arrested dancing of the newly forming "modern" dance that occurred during the early years of the twentieth century.

One more question remains about this revolution in dancing: What about this dancing attracted visual artists and art critics, such as Caffin and Flitch, to this phenomenon? When our dancer-writers consider their dancing, they do so most often from the physical, kinesthetic viewpoint of the participant, from inside the dancer's experience. The new form of dance attracted visual artists and pictorial photographers for its revolutionary *visual* characteristics that greatly contrasted with the traditional ballet or the entertainment forms of dance they had grown accustomed to seeing. Their training in drawing and painting the human body, the most studied form in art, enabled them to recognize the revolution occurring in dance. The visual features of early modern dance: the simple Greek tunic, the elegantly bare stage, the abstract classical music, and the identifiable emotional message paralleled their own shifting aesthetic and new visual vocabulary. Since the new dance form emphasized motion and not positions—photographers, art critics, and dancers called it the "art of danc-ing"—they were captivated by the motion, the "-ing," of it. It paralleled their contemporary experience of increased speed in transportation, communica-tion, learning, and in life itself. Even if a photograph captures only a single moment in a dance, the photographers who took pictures of dancing helped document this formative period in modern dance. And the dancer-writers who wrote books to explain and sell their revolutionary art-in-the-making took full advantage of the interest and attention of the photographers.

In addition to the use of photographs to illustrate their art, recurring themes appear in the writings about dancing by Isadora Duncan, Raymond Duncan, Mary Beegle, Helen Moller, Eleanor Elder, Margaret H'Doubler, and Margaret Morris. They focus on the activity of dancing for its life-enhancing value, as a harmonious, creative, and expressive art activity. Dancing serves as a metaphor for a good life. They all see rhythm as the binding force, running through and organizing dancing and the other arts. This rhythm, found in nature, ties the creative arts to the earth's natural forces, and reflects the unified vision they each hold of human beings, the arts, and the universe. Dancing is best done out of doors in nature, and everyone can participate. They all stress amateur, not professional, participation. The participants compose the dances, and the dancing they perform must reflect the contemporary context and fit the people's highest needs. Our authors see dancing as a treasured educational activity which can elevate the tastes of the common people to appreciate the finer things in life.

The concepts the dancer-writers articulate must be placed into their social-political context. Recently scholars have reexamined what came to be known after World War I as the "progressive" agenda. Though this agenda began in separate fields by several people for different reasons, the backgrounds of these people had shared salient features. The reformers themselves came mostly from upper middle-class or upper-class backgrounds and most graduated from colleges or universities. In the early twentieth century they represented a distinct minority. They assumed their vision of the arts, their concept of society, and their use of leisure time and extra money was correct—and therefore could satisfy the life goals of all people.

Besides their shared aesthetic background, the dancer-writers shared a similar mind-set. The messages in their books essentially preached to the converted; they addressed the people who could afford to purchase their books. The average wage of workers in the early part of the century ranged from $5 to $10 a week. Whereas a movie cost a nickel or a dime, a ticket to the theater cost $2. Helen Moller's book sold for $6. The women who attended the schools of Hellen Moller, Raymond Duncan, and Margaret Morris had leisure time for regular study above and beyond their other schooling. Although Isadora Duncan established her schools for poor children and Margaret Morris had scholarship students, most of the other students of early modern dance had money enough to pay the tuition to attend these schools. So too, the women attending college during this period came from families who could afford to send their daughters to college. From this evidence, we can infer that the participants in early modern dance came from upper-middle and upper-class families. This further explains their rejection of the lower-class jazz, a phenomenon which changed in the 1930s as African-American cultural influences became more widespread and accepted at all levels of American and even British society.

At the end of this century most modern dance instruction occurs mainly in college and university dance departments. Recently modern dance as a creative individualized dance activity has had limited appeal in a culture more and more influenced by activities sponsored by popular and mass media. With the popularity of Music Television (MTV) the visual arts again are affecting the public's view of dancing. The partnership of dance with the visual image—

paintings, lithographs, photographs, motion pictures, or videos—continues with complex and unpredictable results. In spite of technological progress, we hope dancing will continue to play a vital part in this partnership of mixed media.

About the Plates

Plates 1-50 are grouped by the books of dance theory analyzed in Chapters 2-8. To give the reader the sense of opening each book, the title page of each introduces a series of four or five selected photographs. Plates 51-89, referred to in Chapter 10, combine drawings and photographs from several technique books to demonstrate and corroborate the impression given by the photographs in the books containing dance theory.

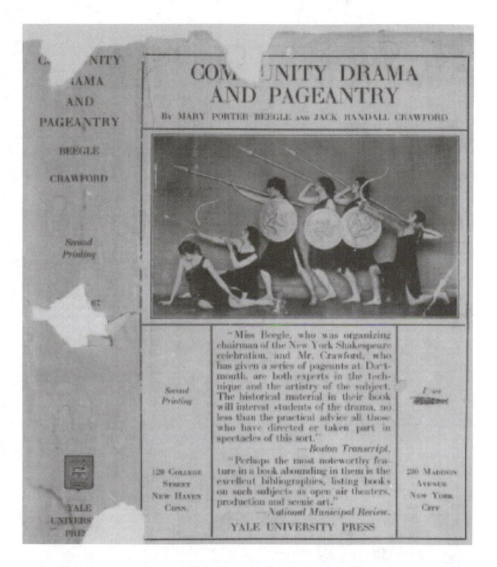

Plate 1. Book jacket of *Community Drama and Pageantry,* 1916. The authors do not include this jacket photograph in the book. Note the balanced yet asymmetrical positions of the groups of pageant participants.

COMMUNITY DRAMA
AND
PAGEANTRY

BY
MARY PORTER BEEGLE
AND
JACK RANDALL CRAWFORD

NEW HAVEN: YALE UNIVERSITY PRESS
LONDON: HUMPHREY MILFORD
OXFORD UNIVERSITY PRESS
MDCCCCXVI

Plate 2. Title page of *Community Drama and Pageantry,* by Mary Porter Beegle and Jack Randall Crawford.

Plate 3. Two photographs from *Community Drama and Pageantry*. Note outdoor settings, Greek tunics as the dancers' costumes, balanced asymmetrical groupings and the distance from which the photographs are shot.

Plate 4. Two photographs by Ira Hill, New York from *Community Drama and Pageantry*. Note Greek tunics and natural outdoor or unadorned indoor settings.

Plate 5. Photograph by A.B. Street from *Community Drama and Pageantry*. Note outdoor setting, Greek costume plus wing-like fabric sleeves, and movement of running or skipping variation with leg back.

Plate 6. Photographs by Ira Hill from *Community Drama and Pageantry*. Note indoor setting in front of a Greek courtyard and outdoor setting from Plate 4, with Greek tunic costumes and asymmetric groupings.

THE DANCE

AND

ITS PLACE IN EDUCATION

With Suggestions and Bibliography
for the Teacher of the Dance

BY

MARGARET NEWELL H'DOUBLER, M. A.

ASSOCIATE PROFESSOR IN
THE DEPARTMENT OF PHYSICAL EDUCATION
UNIVERSITY OF WISCONSIN

NEW YORK
HARCOURT, BRACE AND COMPANY

Plate 7. Title page from *The Dance and Its Place in Education*, 1925, by Margaret Newell H'Doubler.

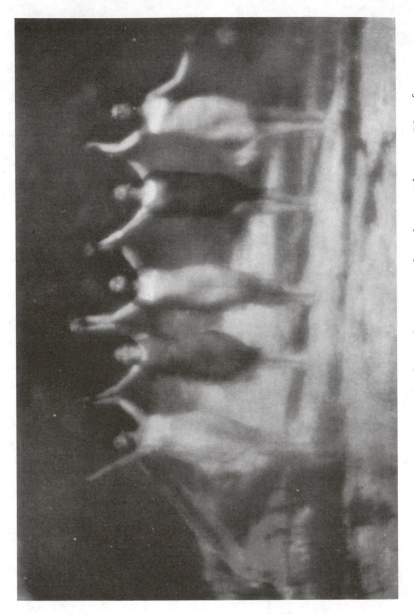

Plate 8. Photograph by George Bell from *The Dance and Its Place in Education*. Note fuzzy background, outdoor setting, Greek costume, and asymmetric grouping.

Plate 9. Photograph by George Bell from *The Dance and Its Place in Education*. Note unadorned indoor setting, Greek costumes, asymmetric grouping, and the distance from which the photograph is shot.

Plate 10. Photograph by George Bell from *The Dance and Its Place in Education*. Note outdoor setting, fuzzy background, Greek costume, and exaggerated skipping position.

Plate 11. Photograph by George Bell from *The Dance and Its Place in Education*. Note fuzzy background, restful natural setting, asymmetrical grouping, and the quietly active poses of the dancers dressed in their Greek costumes.

Dancing with Helen Moller

Her Own Statement of Her Philosophy and Practice
and Teaching Formed upon the Classic Greek
Model, and Adapted to Meet the
Aesthetic and Hygienic
Needs of To-Day

With forty-three full page Art Plates

Edited by
CURTIS DUNHAM

And with an Introduction by
IVAN NARODNY
Author of "The Dance," Department Editor of "The Art of Music"

NEW YORK: JOHN LANE COMPANY
LONDON: JOHN LANE, THE BODLEY HEAD
MCMXVIII

Plate 12. Title page from *Dancing with Helen Moller* edited by Curtis Dunham,
1918.

Plate 13. Photograph from *Dancing with Helen Moller*. Note painting-like quality, arched frame, Greek costume, natural outdoor setting, and arm position seen in photographs of dancers in the books by Beegle and Crawford and H'Doubler.

Plate 14. Photograph from *Dancing with Helen Moller.* Caption reads "An adaption of the classic idea of Pan—three manifestations emphasizing the gay and mischievous attributes of that minor diety of the Arcadian woodland" (p. 28).

Plate 15. Photograph from *Dancing with Helen Moller*. Note unadorned indoor setting, opaque draped cloth as costume, and body position in a skipping variation.

Plate 16. Action photograph at seashore from *Dancing with Helen Moller.* Note running, leaping body position. Caption reads, "The ocean beach upon which the surf rolls rhythmically, or is broken upon half submerged rocks, incites to the most open free and vital dancing expression" (p. 86).

Plate 17. Photograph from *Dancing with Helen Moller.* Note exaggerated skipping position similar to the H'Doubler photograph, Plate 10.

CONTENTS

Plate 18. Table of Contents of *Margaret Morris Dancing* by Margaret Morris and Fred Daniels, 1926. Note generous use of white space typical of the layout throughout the book.

Plate 19. Photograph by Fred Daniels from *Margaret Morris Dancing*. Note outdoor setting, fuzzy background, thin, flowing and revealing costume, and exaggerated backward-leaning skipping position.

Plate 20. Photograph by Fred Daniels from *Margaret Morris Dancing*. Note seashore setting, asymmetrical grouping, exaggerated backward-leaning skipping position, and Margaret Morris's bathing suit with skirt costume.

Plate 21. Photograph by Fred Daniels from *Margaret Morris Dancing*. Note outdoor setting, MM costume, and acrobatic body positions.

Plate 22. Photograph by Fred Daniels from *Margaret Morris Dancing*. Note outdoor setting, symmetrical grouping, and costume: the skirt opens out to look like petals of a flower and the hats look like the center of the flower

Plate 23. Photograph by Fred Daniels from *Margaret Morris Dancing*. Note outdoor setting and exaggerated backwards-leaning skipping positions.

Plate 24. Book cover of *Dancing and Dancers of Today* by Caroline and Charles
H. Caffin, 1912. Note design similar to those on *Camera Works* cover, Plate 25.

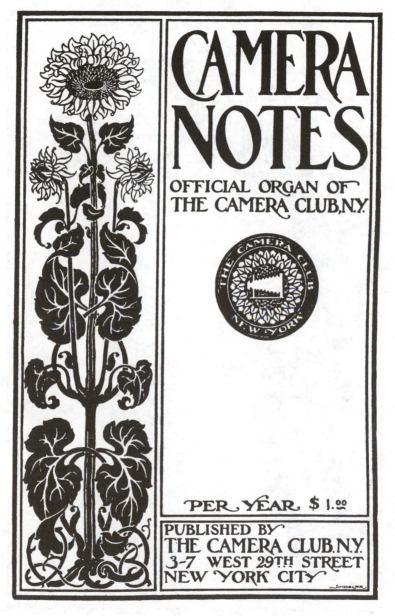

Plate 25. Cover of *Camera Notes*, with decorative floral drawing, Vol. 1, no. 1, 1897.

Plate 26. Cover of *Camera Works*, with drawing by Marius De Zayas, 1910.

Dancing and Dancers of Today

The Modern Revival of Dancing as an Art

BY

CAROLINE AND CHARLES H. CAFFIN

WITH NUMEROUS ILLUSTRATIONS

NEW YORK

Dodd, Mead and Company

1912

Plate 27. Title page of *Dancing and Dancers of Today* by Caroline and Charles H. Caffin, 1912.

Plate 28. Photograph by Jessie Tarbox Beals, a Photo-Secessionist, from *Dancing and Dancers of Today*. Note outdoor setting, Greek tunic costume, and body position similar to the dancers in Plate 16.

Plate 29. Photograph by Clarence White of Gertrude Hoffman's Russian Ballet production from *Dancing and Dancers of Today*. Note held skipping position similar to Plates 10 and 14. As ballet dancers they do not appear to be highly trained, otherwise their positions would be much more precise and similar to one another.

Plate 30. Photograph by Clarence White of Gertrude Hoffman's Russian Ballet production from *Dancing and Dancers of Today.*

Plate 31. Photograph by Clarence White of Gertrude Hoffman's Russian Ballet production from *Dancing and Dancers of Today*. Two dancers still have their wristwatches on their left wrists.

Plate 32. Photograph by Franz Grainer of Rita Saccheto from *Dancing and Dancers of Today*. The photograph is constructed to appear like a painted portrait. Note open book on the window sill and ivy hung to appear like an outdoor setting.

Plate 33. Photograph on the book cover of *Modern Dancing and Dancers* by John Ernest Crawford Flitch, 1912. This photograph also serves as the frontispiece.

MODERN DANCING AND DANCERS

BY

J. E. CRAWFORD FLITCH, M.A.

AUTHOR OF "MEDITERRANEAN MOODS"

WITH EIGHT ILLUSTRATIONS IN COLOUR AND MANY
IN BLACK AND WHITE

PHILADELPHIA

J. B. LIPPINCOTT COMPANY

LONDON: GRANT RICHARDS LTD.

MDCCCCXII

Plate 34. Title page of *Modern Dancing and Dancers* by John Ernest Crawford Flitch, 1912.

Plate 35. Photograph: Dover Street Studios of a young Isadora Duncan from *Modern Dancing and Dancers*. Note pose near a Greek column, Greek costume, and sandal on the foot.

Plate 36. Photograph: Foulsham and Banfield, Ltd. of a young Maud Allan from *Modern Dancing and Dancers*. Note long flowing Greek-like robe and pose similar to those in other photographs.

Plate 37. Photograph of Ruth St. Denis from *Modern Dancing and Dancers*.
Note unusual costume with lots of arm bracelets and bells on her ankles.

Plate 38. Photograph by Bert of "Waslaw (usually Vaslav) Nijinsky from *Modern Dancing and Dancers*. Note his asymmetrical pose.

Plate 39. Photograph by Bert of Tamar Karsavina from *Modern Dancing and Dancers*. Note her asymmetrical pose and heeled shoes.

THE BOOK OF THE DANCE
ARNOLD GENTHE

INTERNATIONAL PUBLISHERS
Eight Beacon Street   -   -   Boston, Massachusetts
1920

Plate 40. Title page for *The Book of the Dance* by Arnold Genthe, 1920.

Plate 41. Photograph by Genthe of Anna Pavlowa (usually Pavlova) from *The Book of the Dance*. Note loose flowing dress, headband, bare feet, and exaggerated skipping position.

Plate 42. Photograph by Genthe of Helen Herendeen from the Biyar School from *The Book of the Dance*. Note the Greek costume and the body position similar to dancers in Plates 16, 28, and 36.

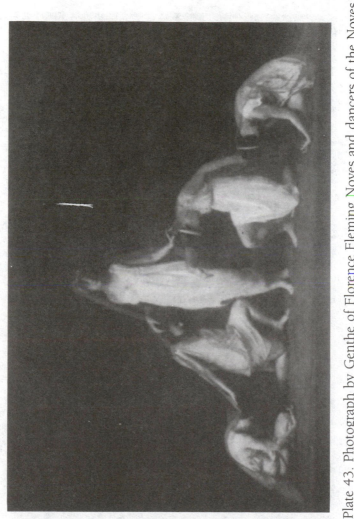

Plate 43. Photograph by Genthe of Florence Fleming Noyes and dancers of the Noyes School from *The Book of the Dance*. Note the Greek costumes and the slightly asymmetric grouping.

Plate 44. Photograph by Genthe of Dulce Moore, a Morgan dancer from *The Book of the Dance*. Note the Greek costume, headband, and exaggerated backward-leaning skipping position.

Plate 45. Photograph by Genthe of Morgan dancers from *The Book of the Dance*. Note the Greek costume, headband, and body positions similar to Beegle's dancers in her pageant dance, Plate 28.

Plate 46. Photograph by Genthe of Hilda Biyar from *The Book of the Dance*. Note the Greek costume, headband, and exaggerated forward-leaning skipping position.

Plate 47. Photograph by Genthe of Liesel of the Duncan School from *The Book of the Dance*. Note the Greek costume, and the exaggerated skipping position with wide-reaching arms similar to the others in this series of photographs.

Plate 48. Photograph by Genthe of Lady Constance Stewart Richardson from *The Book of the Dance*. Note the filmy draped dress, the careful tip-toe walk, and coquettish backward glance.

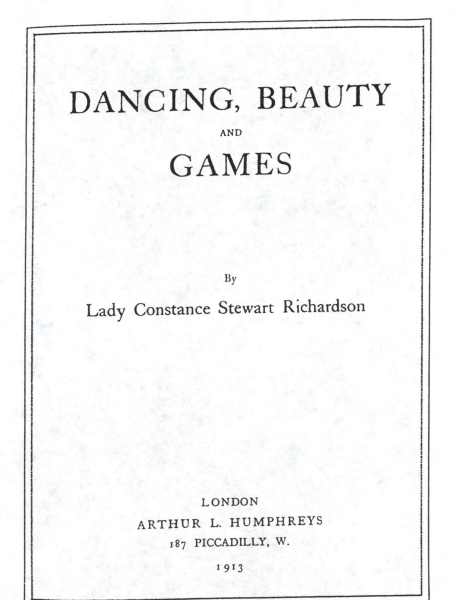

Plate 49. Title page from *Dancing, Beauty, and Games* by Lady Constance
Stewart Richardson, 1913.

Plate 50. Photograph by Clarence White of Lady Constance Stewart Richardson from *Dancing, Beauty, and Games*. Note the light filmy dress and the bent-forward exaggerated skipping position.

MANUAL OF
Gymnastic Dancing

S. C. STALEY, B.P.E., M.A.
and
D. M. LOWERY

ADOPTED BY THE
Y. M. C. A. PHYSICAL DIRECTORS' SOCIETY

A slight reconstruction of a thesis presented to the faculty
of the Y. M. C. A. College of Springfield, Mass., by S. C.
Staley in the year 1917, in partial fulfilment of the require-
ments for the degree of Bachelor of Physical Education.

PRINTED WITH THE PERMISSION OF
THE Y. M. C. A. COLLEGE OF SPRINGFIELD, MASS.

ASSOCIATION PRESS
NEW YORK: 347 MADISON AVENUE

Plate 51. Title page of *Manual of Gymnastic Dancing* by S.C. Staley and D.M. Lowery, 1920.

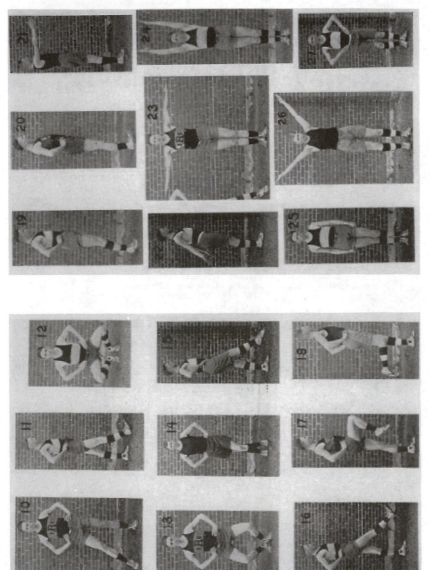

Plate 52. Eighteen photographs of the positions of the feet and legs (10-20), positions of the arms and hands (21-27), from *Manual of Gymnastic Dancing*. Note the leg positions especially in no. 17 and 18.

METROPOLITAN CULTURE SERIES.

✳

THE DELSARTE SYSTEM

OF

PHYSICAL CULTURE.

FIRST EDITION.

NEW YORK:
THE BUTTERICK PUBLISHING COMPANY.(LIMITED).
1893.

Plate 53. Title page of *The Delsarte System of Physical Culture* by Eleanor Georgen, 1893.

FIGURE No. 100.

FIGURE No. 99.

FIGURE No. 101.

FIGURE No. 98.

Plate 54. Principal oppositions between the body and arms, first to fourth, from *The Delsarte System of Physical Culture*, figures no. 98, 99, 100, 101. Note similarity to some of the dancers' positions in the preceding photographs.

FIGURE No. 102.

FIGURE No. 103.

FIGURE No. 104.

FIGURE No. 105.

Plate 55. Principal oppositions between the body and arms, fifth to eighth, from *The Delsarte System of Physical Culture*, figures no. 102, 103, 104, 105.

FIGURE No. 106.   FIGURE No. 107.   FIGURE No. 108.

FIGURE No. 109.   FIGURE No. 111.   FIGURE No. 110.

Plate 56. Principal oppositions between the body and arms, ninth to fourteenth, from *The Delsarte System of Physical Culture*, figures no. 106, 107, 108, 109, 110, 111.

THE ART OF DANCING

ITS

THEORY AND PRACTICE

By F. Leslie Clendenen.
Drawings by Mrs. Clendenen.

Intended for Amateurs as well as for:

Professional Teachers in Schools, Colleges, Seminaries
or Academies, where Dancing and Health
Culture are Taught.

Fully Explaining the Foundation and How to Teach, Interpretative, Classic, Pantomime, Egyptian, Greek, and Toe
Dancing. Also Health Dancing and Exercises.

Plate 57. Title page of *The Art of Dancing: Its Theory and Practice* by F. Leslie Clendenen, 1919.

INTERPRETATIVE POSINGS

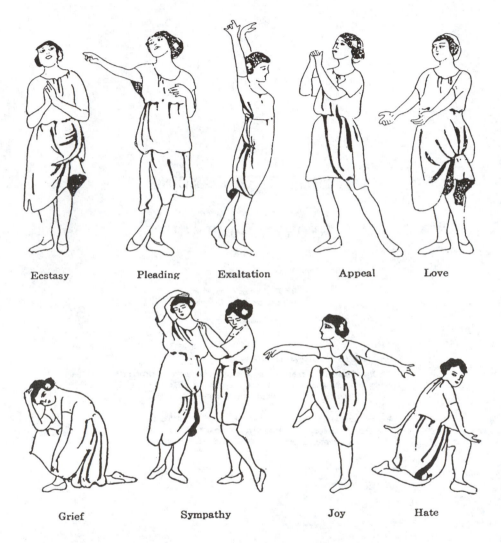

Ecstasy	Pleading	Exaltation	Appeal	Love

Grief	Sympathy	Joy	Hate

Plate 58. Interpretive posings based on Delsarte positions in *The Art of Dancing: Its Theory and Practice* . Note the body position of "joy" and compare it to the forward-leaning exaggerated skipping position seen frequently in the preceding photographs.

The Technique
of
Isadora Duncan

By
Irma Duncan

Illustrated

Kamin Publishers

Plate 59. Title page of *The Technique of Isadora Duncan* by Irma Duncan, 1937.

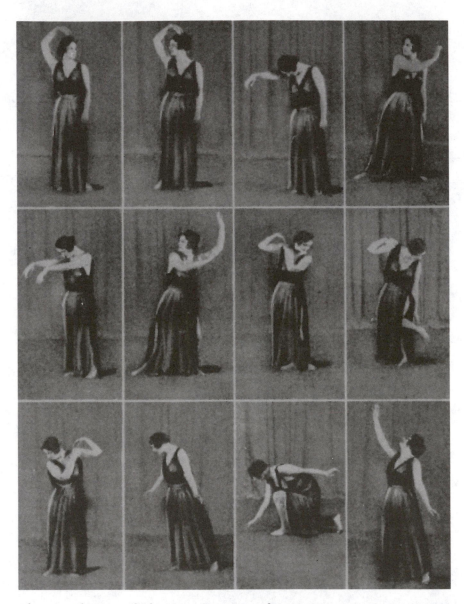

Plate 60. Photographs by Hans V. Briesen of Irma Duncan in Tanagra Figures from *The Technique of Isadora Duncan*. Compare to Plates 54, 55, 56, and 58. Note how the Delsarte oppositions were adapted for "natural dancing."

DANCE, A NATIONAL ART

BY

ELEANOR ELDER

THEOSOPHICAL PUBLISHING HOUSE
ADYAR, MADRAS, INDIA
T. P. H., LONDON, BENARES, KROTONA, U.S.A.
INDIAN BOOK DEPOT, BOMBAY
1918

Plate 61. Title page of *Dance, A National Art* by Eleanor Elder, 1918.

Plate 62. Photograph of Raymond Duncan's first Greek Dance Position from *Dance, A National Art*.

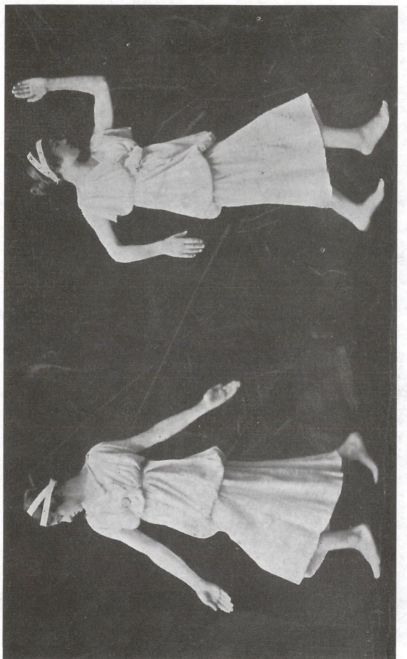

Plate 63. Photograph of Raymond Duncan's second and third Greek Dance Position from *Dance, A National Art*.

Plate 64. Photograph of Raymond Duncan's fourth and fifth Greek Dance Position from *Dance, A National Art*.

Plate 65. Photograph of Raymond Duncan's sixth Greek Dance Position from *Dance, A National Art*.

Plate 66. Photograph of Women Harvesters round the Altar, taken in India, from *Dance, A National Art*. Note outdoor setting, Greek costumes, and symmetrical grouping.

Plate 67. Photograph of Entrance of the Harvesters, taken in India, from *Dance, A National Art*. Note outdoor setting, Greek costumes, and symmetrical grouping.

Design No. 1   No. 2

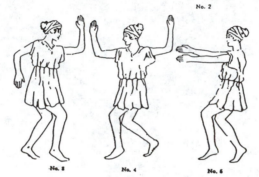

-No. 3   No. 4   No. 5

Fifty

No. 6
GREEK DESIGNS.

Plate 68. The six original Greek positions from *The Art of Dancing: Its Theory and Practice* by F. Leslie Clendenen. Compare to photographs of Raymond Duncan's Greek positions, Plates 62-65.

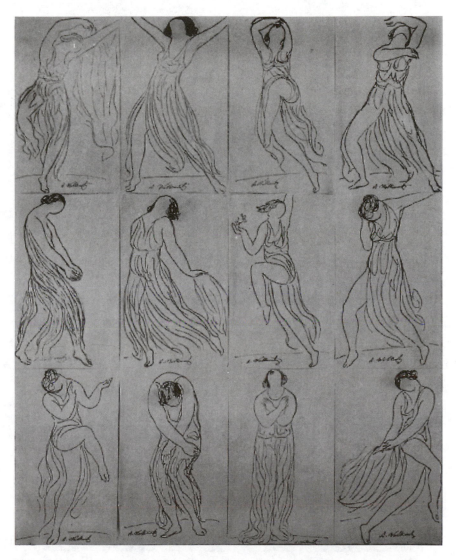

Plate 69. Pen and ink drawings of Isadora Duncan by Abraham Walkowitz, 1920.

Plate 70. Pastel sketches of Isadora Duncan by Maurice Denis, 1910.

I. Types of Skip

Plate 71. Types of skip from *Eurhythmics, Art and Education* by Jaques-Dalcroze 1935. Compare to the many dancers in these skipping positions in the preceding photographs and drawings.

Plate 72. Photograph of Duncan pupil by Hans V. Briesen from *The Technique of Isadora Duncan* found in Lesson 3, "Skipping." Note similarities to Dalcroze variations of a skip, Plate 71.

Plate 73. Photograph of Duncan pupil by Hans V. Briesen from *The Technique of Isadora Duncan* found in Lesson 4, "The Swingstep." Note similarities to Dalcroze variations of a skip, Plate.71.

RHYTHM, MUSIC AND EDUCATION

BY

EMILE JAQUES-DALCROZE

TRANSLATED FROM THE FRENCH
BY HAROLD F. RUBINSTEIN

ILLUSTRATED

G. P. PUTNAM'S SONS
NEW YORK AND LONDON
The Knickerbocker Press
1921

Plate 74. Title page of *Rhythm, Music, and Education* by Emile Jaques-Dalcroze, 1921.

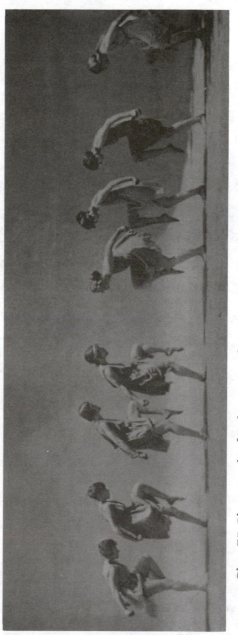

Plate 75. Photograph of Dalcroze pupils in an essay, "Eurhythmics and Musical Composition" (1915). Note Greek costume and bent-over skipping position.

Plate 76. Photographs of Dalcroze pupils in an essay, "Music and the Dancer" (1918). Note similarities to the dancers in these positions in the preceding photographs.

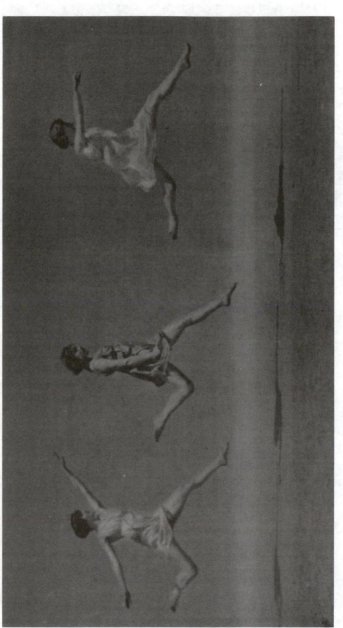

Plate 77. Photograph of Dalcroze pupils leaping placed in an essay "Rhythm and Gesture in Music Drama—and Criticism" (1910–1916) in *Rhythm, Music, and Education.*

Plate 78. Photograph of Dalcroze pupils leaping placed in an essay "How to Revive Dancing" (1912) in *Rhythm, Music, and Education.*

Plate 79. Photograph of Duncan pupil by Hans V. Briesen in Lesson No. 5, "Jumping" in *The Technique of Isadora Duncan*. Note similarities to Dalcroze's photographs of leaping, Plates 77, 78.

THE IMPORTANCE OF BEING RHYTHMIC

A STUDY OF THE PRINCIPLES OF DALCROZE
EURYTHMICS APPLIED TO GENERAL EDUCA-
TION AND TO THE ARTS OF MUSIC, DANCING
AND ACTING. BASED ON AND ADAPTED
FROM "RHYTHM, MUSIC AND EDUCATION,"
BY ÉMILE JAQUES-DALCROZE

BY

JO PENNINGTON

WITH AN INTRODUCTION BY
WALTER DAMROSCH

DRAWINGS BY THE LATE PAUL THEVENAZ
PHOTOGRAPHS BY EDWIN F. TOWNSEND, NEW YORK

G. P. Putnam's Sons
New York & London
The Knickerbocker Press
1925

Plate 80. Title page of *The Importance of Being Rhythmic* by Jo Pennington (1925).

Plate 81. Drawings of a crescendo exercise from Dalcroze Eurhythmics in *The Importance of Being Rhythmic*.

Plate 82. Photograph of crescendo of movement placed in "An Essay in the Reform of Music Teaching in Schools" (1905) by Dalcroze from *Rhythm, Music, and Education*. Note similarity to Pennignton's drawings in Plate 81.

Plate 83. Photograph of crescendo and diminuendo by a group from *The Importance of Being Rhythmic.*

A MANUAL OF DANCING

Suggestions and Bibliography
for the teacher of dancing

By
MARGARET N. H'DOUBLER, B. A.

Assistant Professor in the
Department of Physical Education
University of Wisconsin

Madison, Wisconsin
1921

Plate 84. Title page of *A Manual of Dancing* by Margaret N. H'Doubler, 1921.

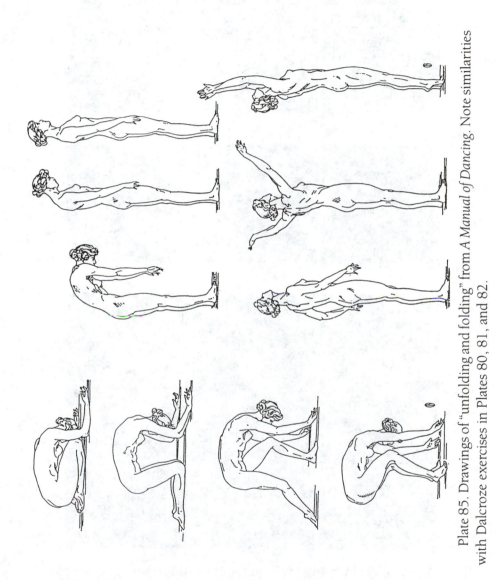

Plate 85. Drawings of "unfolding and folding" from *A Manual of Dancing*. Note similarities with Dalcroze exercises in Plates 80, 81, and 82.

Plate 86. Photograph of Irma Duncan by Hans V. Briesen of Lesson No. 7, "Lying Down and Rising." Note similarities to Dalcroze exercise in Plates 81, 82, 83, and H'Doubler's "unfolding and folding" in Plate 85.

Plate 87. Photograph of Dalcroze pupil performing four skipping steps from *The Importance of Being Rhythmic*. Note similarities to preceding photographs of dancers performing variations on skipping.

Plate 88. Photograph of Dalcroze pupils in two groupings from *The Importance of Being Rhythmic*. Note similarities to preceding photographs of dancers in Plates 4, 6, and 30.

Plate 89. Photograph of Dalcroze pupil demonstrating "Eurhythmics in the Use of the Body as a Musical Instrument" from *The Importance of Being Rhythmic*. Note strength of gesture and short-skirted costume similar to Margaret Morris's dance costume.

References

Alter, Judith B. (1991) *Dance-Based Dance Theory: From Borrowed Models to Dance-Based Experience.* New York and Bern, Switzerland: Peter Lang Publishers.

————. (1984) "Music and Rhythm in Dance: H'Doubler's Views in Retrospect." *Proceedings: Dance History Scholars, Seventh Annual Conference*, Goucher College, Towson, Md, February.

Barzun, Jacques and Henry F. Graff. (1985) *The Modern Researcher.* 4th ed. New York: Harcourt, Brace, Jovanovich, Publishers.

Beaumont, Cyril W. (1966) *A Bibliography of the Dance Collection of Doris Niles and Serge Leslie.* London: C.W. Beaumont.

Beaumont, Cyril W. (1963) *A Bibliography of Dancing.* New York: Benjamin Blom.

Beegle, Mary Porter and John Randall Crawford. (1916) *Community Drama and Pageantry.* New Haven, Conn.: Yale University Press.

Broecker, William L., ed. (1984) *International Center of Photography: Encyclopedia of Photography.* New York: Crown Publishers, Inc.

Brown, Margaret C. and Betty K. Sommer. (1969) *Movement Education: Its Evolution and a Modern Approach.* Reading, Mass.: Addison-Wesley Publishing Company.

Caffin, Caroline. (1914) *Vaudeville.* New York: Kennerly.

Caffin, Caroline and Charles. (1912) *Dancing and Dancers of Today: The Modern Revival of Dancing as an Art.* New York: Dodd, Mead and Co.

Caffin, Charles. (1908) *The Appreciation of Drama.* New York: The Barker and Taylor Company.

Chuyjoy, Anatole. (1949) *The Dance Encyclopedia.* New York: A.S. Barnes and Company.

Chujoy Anatole and P. W. Manchester. (1967) *The Dance Encyclopedia*, revised and enlarged. New York: Simon and Schuster.

Clarke, Mary, and David Vaughn, eds. (1977) *The Enclyclopedia of Dance and Ballet*. New York: G. P. Putnam's Son.

Clendenen, F. Leslie. (1919) *The Art of Dancing: Its Theory and Practice*. St. Louis: F. Leslie Clendenen.

Coben, Stanley. (1991) *Rebellion Against Victorianism: The Impetus for Cultural Change in the 1920s America*. New York: Oxford University Press.

Cohen, Barbara Naomi. (1977) "The Borrowed Art of Gertrude Hoffmann." *Dance Data* Number 2. Brooklyn, N. Y.: Dance Horizons.

Colby, Gertrude R. (1924) *Natural Rhythms and Dances*. New York: A. S. Barnes and Co.

Dewey, John. (1916) *Democracy and Education*. New York: Macmillan Publishing Co. Inc.

Doty, Robert. (1960) *Photo Secession: Photography as a Fine Art*. Monograph no. 1. Rochester, N.Y.: George Eastman House.

Dulles, Foster Rhea. (1965) *A History of Recreation: America Learns to Play*. New York: Appleton-Century-Crofts.

Duncan, Irma. (1937) *The Technique of Isadora Duncan*. New York: Kamin Publishers.

_____. (1966) *Duncan Dancer: An Autobiography*. Middleton, Conn.: Wesleyan University Press.

Duncan, Isadora. (1927) *My Life*. New York: Boni and Liveright.

_____. (1928) *The Art of the Dance*. New York: Helen Hackett Inc. Reprinted 1969. Ed. Sheldon Cheney, New York: Theatre Arts Books.

Duncan, Raymond. "La Danse et La Gymnastique." Conférence faite le 4 Mai, 1914 à L'Université hellenique Salle de Geographie, Paris, Akademia Raymond Duncan. Translated Glenna Josephson, 1990.

Egbert, Donald Drew. (1970) *Social Radicalism and the Arts: Western Europe. A Cultural History from the French Revolution to 1968.* New York: Alfred A. Knopf.

Elder, Eleanor. (1918) *Dance, A National Art.* Adyar, Madras, India: Theosophical Publishing House.

Ewing, William A. (1987) *Dance and Photography.* New York: Henry Holt and Company.

Fleming, William. (1970) *Art, Music, and Ideas.* New York: Holt, Rinehart and Winston, Inc.

Flitch, J. E. Crawford. (1912) *Modern Dancing and Dancers.* Philadelphia: J.B. Lippincott Co.

Franklin, Fay, ed. (1981) *History's Timeline.* New York: Crescent Books.

Gadan, Francis, Robert Maillard, and Selma Jeanne Cohen. (1959) *Dictionary of Modern Ballet.* New York: Tudor Publishing Company.

Genthe, Arnold. (1916) *The Book of the Dance.* Boston: International Publishers.

Georgen, Eleanor. (1893) *The Delsarte System of Physical Culture.* New York: The Butterick Publishing Company.

Gerber, Ellen W. (1971) *Innovators and Institutions in Physical Education.* Philadelphia: Lea and Febiger.

Golby, J.M. and Purdue, A.W. (1985) *The Civilization of the Crowd: Popular Culture in England,1750-1900.* New York: Schocken Books.

Goldschmidt, Lucien. (1980) *The Truthful Lens: A Survey of the Photographically Illustrated Book, 1844-1914.* New York: Grolier Club.

Green, Jonathan. (no date) *A Critical Anthology of CAMERA WORK* (pamphlet in the special collections section in the University of California-Los Angeles Research Library).

Gutek, Gerals L. (1986) *Education in the United States: An Historical Perspective*. Englewood Cliffs, N.J.: Prentice-Hall.

H'Doubler, Margaret Newell. (1921) *A Manual of Dancing: Suggestions and Bibliography for the Teacher of Dancing*. Madison, Wisc.: self-published.

_____. (1940) *Dance: A Creative Art Experience*. New York: F. S. Crofts and Company.

_____. (1925) *The Dance and Its Place in Education*. New York: Harcourt, Brace and Company.

Hackensmith, C. W. (1966) *History of Physical Education*. New York: Harper and Row, Publishers.

Hall, G. Stanley. (1911) *Educational Problems*. Vol. 1. New York: D. Appleton and Company.

Hutchinson-Guest, Ann. (1984) *Dance Notation: The Process of Recording Dance on Paper*. New York: Dance Horizons.

Jaques-Dalcroze, Emile. (1921) "How to Revive Dancing." (1912) in *Rhythm, Music and Education*. Harold, F. Rubinstein, trans. New York: G.P. Putnam's Sons.

Jenkyns, Richard. (1980) *The Victorians and Ancient Greece*. Oxford: Basil Blackwell.

Johnson, Allen, ed. (1929) *Dictionary of American Biography*. New York: Charles Scribner's Sons.

Kendall, Elizabeth. (1979) *Where She Danced*. New York: Alfred A. Knopf.

Koegler, Horst. (1977) *The Concise Oxford Dictionary of Ballet*. London: Oxford University Press.

Kraus, Richard and Sara A. Chapman. (1981) *History of the Dance in Art and Education*. 2nd ed. Englewood Cliffs, N.J: Prentice-Hall.

Lane, Michael. (1980) *Books and Publishers: Commerce Against Culture in Postwar Britain.* Lexington, Mass.: D.C. Heath and Company.

Larkin, Oliver W. (1960) *Art and Life in America.* New York: Holt, Rinehart and Winston.

Lehmann-Haupt, Helmut. (1939) *The Book in America, A History of the Making, the Selling and the Collecting of Books in the United States.* New York: R.R. Bowker Co.

Loewenthal, Lillian. (1993) *The Search for Isadora: The Legend and Legacy of Isadora Duncan.* Princeton, N.J.: Dance Horizons, Princeton Book Company.

Madison, Charles A. (1966) *Book Publishing in America.* New York: McGraw-Hill Book Co.

Magriel, Paul D. (1936) *A Bibliography of Dancing,* and (1941) *Fourth cumulated supplement.* New York: H.W. Wilson Co.

————, ed. (1947) Isadora Duncan. New York, Henry Holt and Company.

————. (1977) Nijinsky, Pavlova, Duncan. New York: Da Capo Press.

Martin, John. (1936) *America Dancing: The Background and Personalities of the Modern Dance.* New York: Dodge Publishing Company.

Mayer, Frederick. (1964) *American Ideas and Education.* Columbus, Ohio: Charles E. Merrill Books, Inc.

Mergen, Bernard. (1977) "From Play to Recreation: The Acceptance of Leisure in the United States, 1890-1930" in *Studies in the Anthropology of Play: Papers in Memory of B. Allan Tindall,* ed. Phillips Stevens. West Point, N.Y.: Leisure Press, pp. 55-63.

Miller, Tice L. (1981) *Bohemians and Critics: American Theatre Criticism in the Nineteenth Century.* Metuchen, N.J.: The Scarecrow Press, Inc.

Moller, Helen. (1918) *Dancing with Helen Moller.* ed. Curtis Dunham. New York: John Lane Company.

Clipping file for Helen Moller at Lincoln Center Library of the Performing Arts in New York: "Teachers Grace by 'Natural Dancing'," *Toledo Times*, 5 March 1916; "Outdoor Dancers by the Sea," *Vanity Fair,* July 1916; "Helen Moller" Program announcement for Carnegie Hall, New York, Monday March at 3 p.m. (no year); *Dancing with Helen Moller*, book review, *New York Sun*, 24 March 1918.

Morris, Margaret with Fred Daniels. (1926) *Margaret Morris Dancing*. London: Kegan Paul, Trench, Trubner, and Co. Ltd.

Morris, Margaret. (1969) *My Life in Movement*. London: Peter Owen.

Morrison, Theodore. (1974) *Chautauqua: A Center for Education, Religion, and the Arts in America*. Chicago: The University of Chicago Press.

Munro, Thomas. (1967) *The Arts and Their Interrelationships*. Cleveland, Ohio: The Press of Western Reserve University.

Newhall, Beaumont. (1964) *The History of Photography, from 1839 to the Present Day*. New York: The Museum of Modern Art.

Norrie, Ian. (1982) *Mumby's Publishing and Bookselling in the Twentieth Century*. 6th ed. London: Bell and Hyman.

Ornstein, Allan C. and Daniel U. Levine. (1984) *An Introduction to the Foundations of Education*. Boston: Houghton Mifflin Company.

Panati, Charles. (1991) *Panati's Parade of Fads, Follies, and Manias: The Origins of Our Most Cherished Obsessions*. New York: Harper Collins Publishers.

Parrington, Vernon Louis. (1930) *Main Currents in American Thought: An Interpretation of American Literature from the Beginnings to 1920*. New York: Harcourt, Brace and Company.

Paxton, John and Sheila Fairfield. (1984) *Chronology of Culture: A Chronology of Literature, Dramatic Arts, Music, Architecture, Three-dimensional Art, and Visual Arts from 3000 B.C. to the Present*. New York: Van Nostrand Reinhold Company.

Peiss, Kathy. (1986) *Cheap Amusements: Working Women and Leisure in Turn-of-the-Century New York*. Philadelphia: Temple University Press.

Pennington, Jo. (1925) *The Importance of Being Rhythmic: A Study of the Principles of Dalcroze Eurythmics Applied to General Education and to the Arts of Music, Dancing, and Acting, Based on and Adapted From "Rhythm, Music, and Education" by Emile Jaques-Dalcroze*. New York: G. P. Putnam's Sons.

Percival, John. (1971) *Experimental Dance*. London: Studio Vista.

Prevots, Naima. (1990) *American Pageantry: A Movement for Art and Democracy*. Ann Arbor, Mich: UMI Press.

Raffe, W. G. and M. E. Purdon. (1964) *Dictionary of the Dance*. New York: A. S. Barnes and Company.

Reely, Mary Katharine, ed. (1919) *Book Review Digest*. New York: The H. W. Wilson, Company.

Richardson, Lady Constance Stewart. (1913) *Dancing, Beauty, and Games*. London: Arthur L. Humphreys.

Rogers, Frederick Rand. (1941) *Dance: A Basic Educational Technique: A Functional Approach to the Use of Rhythmics and Dance as Prime Methods of Body Development and Control, and Transformation of Moral and Social Behavior*. New York: The Macmillan Company.

Rosenblum, Naomi. (1989) *A World History of Photography*. New York: Abbeville Press.

Rudofsky, Bernard. (1974) *The Unfashionable Human Body*. New York: Anchor Press, Doubleday Books.

Rushdoony, Rousas J. (1963) *The Messianic Character of American Education*. Nutley, N. J.: The Craig Press.

Ruyter, Nancy Lee C. (1979) *Reformers and Visionaries: The Americanization of the Art of Dance*. New York: Dance Horizons.

Schlereth, Thomas J. (1991) *Victorian America: Transformations in Everyday Life, 1876-1915*. New York: Harper Collins.

Schmitt, Peter J. (1969) *Back to Nature: The Arcadian Myth in Urban America*. New York: Oxford University Press.

Schneider, Ilya Ilyich. (1969) *Isadora Duncan: The Russian Years*. New York: Da Capo Press.

Seroff, Victor. (1971) *The Real Isadora*. New York: The Dial Press.

Smith, F. Seymour. (1964) *Bibliography in the Bookshop*. London: Andre Deutsch.

Smith, Page. (1984) *The Rise of Industrial America: A People's History of the Post-Reconstruction Era*. Vol. 6. London: Penguin Books.

Souriau, Paul. (1983) *The Aesthetics of Movement*. Manon Souriau, trans.. Amherst, Mass.: The University of Massachusetts Press.

Spector, Irwin. (1992) *Rhythm and Life: The Work of Emile Jaques-Dalcroze*. Stuyvesant, N.Y.: Pendragon Press.

Spiesman, Mildred. (1960) "Dance Education Pioneers: Colby, Larson, H'Doubler." *Journal of Health, Physical Education, and Recreation* (January), pp. 25-26,76.

_____. (1951) "The Bird Larson School of Natural Rhythmic Expression." *Dance Magazine*, Vol. 25 (Sept.), pp. 22,35.

Staley, S. C. and Lowery, D. M. (1920) *Manual of Gymnastic Dancing*. New York: Association Press.

Steichen, Edward. (1963) *A Life in Photography*. Garden City, N.Y.: Doubleday and Company.

Stein, Jess, ed. (1983) *The Random House Dictionary of the English Language*. New York: Random House.

Tebbel, John. (1975) *A History of Book Publishing in the United States*, Vol. 2: *The Expansion of an Industry, 1865-1919*. New York: R.R. Bowker.

Urlin, Ethel. (1911) *Dancing: Ancient and Modern.* London: Herbert and Daniel.

Walvin, James. (1987) *Victorian Values.* Athens, Ga.: The University of Georgia Press.

Wingo, G. Max. (1974) *Philosophies of Education: An Introduction.* Lexington, Mass.: D.C. Heath and Company.

Who Was Who in Literature: 1906-1934. (1939) Vol. 1 (A-K) Detroit: Gale Research Company.

Note

Sources consulted to find information about the dance criticism written by Charles and Caroline Caffin and John E. Crawford Flitch: W. G. Raffe and M. E. Purdon; Francis Gadan, Robert Maillard, and Selma Jeanne Cohen; Anatole Chuyjoy; Mary Clarke and David Vaughan; Horst Koegler; and Anatole Chujoy and P. W. Manchester.

Appendix
Dance and Gymnastics

By Raymond Duncan
1914

In the last few years we have witnessed, under the name of physical culture, an attempt at a renaissance of gymnastics. In spite of all the circus atmosphere and all the publicity which has surrounded this movement we can say that all that has been tried until now to get out of the old routines has been rather infantile.

All our systems of physical culture are based on the games of ancient Greece, but in trying to imitate the forms we have neglected the spirit. We wish to develop a classical muscular system while ignoring the classical emotions. The modern discus thrower wants to throw his discus as far as possible and the ancient one with the greatest possible accuracy. The modern runner wishes to arrive the most quickly, and the ancient desired to run with the most beautiful movements.

The modern athlete wants to do something stronger, faster, farther, while the ancient one wanted to express the most beautiful emotions during the exercise. What is called physical culture today is limited to the cultivation of muscles. We forget that the word "physical," properly speaking, means nature, and that the term "physical culture" in reality signifies the cultivation of the entire being: muscles, feeling, mind and soul.

For me the word "gymnastics" does not mean muscular exercise, but human exercise, exercise in which take part at the same time the body and soul, both the muscles and the intelligence. It is not only an exercise or a system which we practice with the aim of acquiring health, beauty of the body, strength or agility: it is the human exercise for attaining life itself, to become truly a human being, to realize an ideal which is worth being lived, finally for becoming a transforming power which by its acts and by its resulting thought exerts a wholesome influence, not only on its fellows but on the earth itself.

For me human beings are instruments, machines which heaven has sent, not to amuse themselves, not to improve themselves, not to become good, healthy, or even righteous, but to work. And it seems to me that when the machines that we are do not work or work badly, we are condemned to suffer. On the contrary, when they work well, they feel nothing but happiness, the emotions, the feelings that are engendered by the movements of the work, in the production of beautiful and necessary things.

True gymnastics is the exercise of natural activities resulting from normal work and from games. But as the world has been decadent for many centuries, a system of gymnastics summarizing the activities of all work becomes necessary to replace defective work activities and to stop the decadence. The reconstruction of this system consists of the production of objects necessary to life and to its development.

We know very well that all that exists on the earth is in motion, that nothing truly dead exists. Death does not exist, or rather is itself in motion. Its manifestation is the expression of a movement of matter. Without the vibrations produced by the electric machine, no light. Without the motion of the winds, the waters which come down from the mountains, the sap which circulates in the veins of the tree, of the little earthworm which stirs the earth in which the tree grows, finally without the movements of the carpenter, we would not have chairs.

Thus, every natural phenomenon is only the result, the expression of a movement. We ourselves are living machines whose role is to spread movement. Our motions are not manifested solely in the external movement of our arms, of our legs, of our bodies; they produce also in us movements of the blood, of the muscles. We have thousands of forms of motion even to those higher movements which are called movements of the soul, of the mind. And if we look at the light we find behind it the movement of the electric machine. If we look at the chair we find behind it the movements of the carpenter, that of the life of the trees, that of the winds. And if we undertake a study of gymnastic, it is not only because we wish to increase or conserve our energies, because we desire that all the parts of our bodies and all our organs constitute a human harmony, but because we want above all to put ourselves in harmony with the movements of our soul, which is itself in direct contact with the divine movement, in order to truly feel, to truly understand, and to truly fulfill our task in the universe well.

All our popular melodies, all the great traditional music that our peoples still sing are only the vocal expression of the movements of dance and gymnastics. All the beauties of character of our peoples are the results of their movements and would become stronger and more exact by means of their repetition and rhythmic formation by the dance.

The highest thought of Socrates, the great ideals of this great man, were only the small effervescence springing from his movements, of his studies of the dance, of gymnastics.

The real Socrates consisted in the movements, the actions of Socrates, and he exists today not because of the persistence of his ideals and of his thoughts, but by the persistence of the movements generated by his movements. And I am sure that without the dance and the gymnastics we would never have had Socrates. Dance and gymnastics, being the resurrection of the movements of the preceding life concentrated in a symmetrical melody, generate a resurrection of the preceding ideals and thoughts in a logical symmetrical form.

And I am sure that without a capacity for rhythmic motion in ourselves we could not sense the truths of Socrates in experiencing the beauties toward which he directs us. In the same way all the beauties of all the divinely great men are more or less lived by us by reason of our capability of responding, of being directed by their movements.

For me, all the sciences are dependent on the idea of movement. Astronomy, the science of the stars, teaches us that the stars are small bodies very far away which go through their trajectories in infinity. Do you think that it would be possible for a great astronomer to make a study of the movement of the stars and to understand it if motion did not exist in him? Do you think that it is possible for an awkward man who walks all bent over, all broken, to feel the beauty of the movement of the stars? Did not Flammarion, at the time when he wrote his best books, still have in him a small memory of the beautiful motions that he made while he was still a child? And do you not think that it would be possible to undertake a study of gymnastics which would give in the movements of the body, external or internal, in the movements of the emotions and of thought, an exact understanding of the movement of the stars a thousand times more precious that all that the astronomers have given us up to now?

Likewise, what use is the study of the earth, the mountains and the volcanoes, of the ocean and of the islands by the great geographers if there does not exist movement in the rivers, in the ocean, in the mountains and volcanoes? What is the good of studying geography if we have not begun by sensing movement, by giving ourselves the illusion of movement with maps, relief maps, maps of the world, accounts of travels, etc., an illusion which has the effect of producing a movement in our bodies and in our souls?

In the same way it is not enough for the great geologists to know the formation of mountains, the advance of waters which run from the mountains to the valleys and from the sea to the mountains, the slow balancing of the earth's crust which is raised here and sinks down farther away; it is also necessary that they feel these great phenomena. But how glimpse the existence of these movements if one does not already have movement in oneself?

We have in Paris great concerts, great orchestras, like the Colonne Orchestra.

The music that they play is motion, a motion very physical; it is not the sounds that the instruments emit. The sounds are only the result of the motion. So you think that we would be able to feel the beauty in the music without having the movement in ourselves?

In the lower schools, the kindergartens invented by Froebel for the very young, from three to six years old, they teach little human activities, little songs, little dances, little games. So you think that in your schools where movement, gymnastics, physical exercise are taught as a remedy and not as a need, the usage of such a system would be capable of generating great sentiments, great emotions, and that those who practiice it would be capable of sensing the great truths of life? . . . Don't you think that if our present humanity has fallen very low, if we find ourselves very ugly, very ill, very stupid, it is because we have not received a good education in motion? We recognize ourselves that an education of motion is quite necessary, but what system to choose?

Many years ago, when I was still a little boy, I understood that without motion we cannot live. They sent me to school, made me sit on a chair to study, to find the difference between A and B; I always felt that I did not like those A's and those B's. They told me: "You must study arithmetic." To which I replied: "I want to play ball with my little comrades." But since everyone stayed at school, I escaped from school, saying to myself: "No, I will be a man! I don't want any more school!" . . Very well! But I must make a living! . . . What to do? I began by learning telegraphy. I remember very well the happiness I felt in making this first study in movement. I was conscious of having obtained a great privilege when I was able to be the first of my team to sit down in front of an aparatus before two in the afternoon and to stay there until the next morning at seven o'clock, making little motions with only one hand. Having two feet and two hands I wondered what inventor could have developed this movement on the instrument. I cried out: "Good Lord! Why then can't I move?" It is very ugly to remain thus making use of only one hand. I do not wish to remain ugly while working at the telegraph. What to do? . . . Work in a printing shop? There they work with both hands. They put thousands of sheets of paper on the hand press. And when I wish to work with both hands my feet in turn insist on movement.

Then I began my studies of movement by trying to cross all of America from San Francisco to New York. I climb a mountain: here is motion. I go down the mountain: here is motion producing heat and fatigue. A large fragment detaches itself from the mountain: here is another movement. And little by little I begin to sense all this great American continent with its mountains and its valleys, its rivers, its plains, and its deserts. I have even found the basis for a great study. The very movement of the earth has transported itself through my body into my soul. Then I began to hear a melody, an extraordinary harmony which awakened in me the desire to hear the same harmony, but symmetrical, well-formed, well-ordered, placed in a framework which would permit me to understnd it better. That is why I began my studies of natural gymnastics, not solely in making the motions for learning gymnastics, but in doing research to understand what gymnastics can be. These researches directed me toward Greece, in the museums. There I found on the painted vases series upon series of motions of which certain ones seemed to me to resemble my own motions when I go up or go down a mountain. The motions of fatigue, of pain, of joy, of majestic strength. I worked years upon years making sketches from these vases until the day when I had before my eyes a vision of all the movements of these vases synthesized in one single great cinematographic movement. Then I had the vision of ancient Greece in motion.

For us the designs and paintings which unfold on these ancient "terra-cottas" are not the models of a precise beauty, they are not only specimens of an artistic or historic value much greater that all the others, they are also almost the sole documents which remain to us of the great tradition of rhythmic movements of the pre-Hellenic and classical eras. What is particularly interesting in this process of decoration on ceramics is the exact idea, that they supply, of the great natural laws.

On these pre-Hellenic vases, which display at the outset only simple geometric designs then little be little are covered with representations of human and animal movements, we find only two angles which are sufficient to express not only all possible movements but the most natural forms of our movements. Continuing, we notice that the more obtuse the angles the less beautiful the forms.

All the designs of antiquity were not decorative designs, imitations of animal or human figures like today, but a means of expressing movements. Unconsciously many children recreate these same archaic designs without however ever before having had their eyes on the models. Our simplified design of art rests on scaffoldings of triangles inscribed within squares, whose composing straight lines serve to create a diagrammatic image of the human body. All our motions which may sometimes seem curved or undulating are in reality models of these figures of angles and of squares.

Having abandoned my studies of Greek vases I went among farmers and workers. I saw blacksmiths striking iron, carpenters sawing or splitting wood. I noticed that the movements of the good workers, of those who manifested health or radiated joy, absolutely resembled the motions that I had seen covering those Greek vases. This observation gave me the idea of beginning the reconstruction of a system of natural gymnastics.

An art whose tradition has been lost since classical antiquity, natural gymnastics that we have succeeded in reconstructing will permit us to arrive easily at all the other arts. This art of the harmonic dance, of a dance composed of simple, easy movements, without pretension as to the effect, this perfectly natural art alone can give us the conception of a truly artistic symmentrical expression resulting from all these human motions. We conceive that dance so understood is something better than movement or than a simple exercise of gymnastics. It can be a means of absorbing the harmonious movements of the Universe while dancing and of dispersing them to the public. Thus, carried away themselves by the rhythm of this dance, the audience will lose the taste for going to see the dancers; it will feel the desire to dance, and will itself learn to dance.

In Epirus, a pastoral country, we have shepherds who live in little villages perched on the mountains. These shepherds have extraordinary emotions. I can show you the emotions of these shepherds when they walk on the mountain, when they assemble around their fire, when they remain seated on the mountain watching the sun. Perhaps then you will begin to have some idea of these emotions. But if I take you there to learn to climb the mountain with the least expenditure of energy, to take care of sheep and goats, to play the flute, to remain seated around a fire with crossed legs to remain on the mountain looking at the stars without using words or movement, to sense the birth of precise thoughts, alone, by yourself, facing the starry night, or again under the burning sun, under the deep blue sky of Greece, with the far-away view of the snowy summits of Pindus, to merge yourself so intimately with that pure air, that azure, thoses rays of sunlight, that snow, those stars, all that will give you pure emotions untranslatable in words!

I don't know why you stay in Paris. What are you doing here? You're working to make a living, aren't you? Take a look at your daily motions! They would be very ugly as movements of dances, wouldn't they? Go to the theater! Look at all the motions that you see there! Imagine them interpreted as dances! Wouldn't it be very ugly? Come with me into the great libraries to translate into dance what we see there! Come with me into our great universities to hear the lectures of the greatest scholars, of the greatest philosophers! It would be ugly, wouldn't it! Then come into our great art schools. Look at the models that they contain. Imagine them translated into dance movements! What a horrible dance! Look at the students! What stupid dances! Then let's go take a walk along the boulevards! Imagine the movements of the roaring autos: Brrrrr! translated into dance! Imagine the fury of the people pressed all around you translated into dances! You could not bear it.

Thus all the luxury of Paris, all the great splendor of Paris, are worth nothing! Come with me to Epirus! We have no autos, not even highways! In spite of the troubled situation of the country you will see there only extraordinary dances! Not a single movement which is not harmonious!

Imagine that we might succeed in introducing the true dance in Paris! We say to our musician artist: play, play well! but dance at the same time! We say to our great singers: sing, sing well! but for the love of God, dance at the same time! To our professors we say: accompany your discourses with dance! While dancing song or words we begin to live them; we begin to understand what one sings or what one says; we begin to live the verbal or musical emotions.

Come with me to Epirus, help me to found a small ideal country which will be a model for the entire world!

Translated by Glenna Josephson, M.A., 1990.

Index

A

academic field of dance, xii, 9, 77
aesthetic intent, 38, 41, 43, 59, 69, 72, 78. *See* emotions, feelings.
aesthetic result, 39, 43, 45, 46, 78, 107. *See* audience.
Allan, Maud, 88, 89, 92, 104, Plate 36
amusement. *See* entertainment
Arcadia (Arcady), 4, 24, 25, 42-43, 48, 79, 124
Art of Dancing: Its Theory and Practice (The), 55, 107, Plates 57, 58, 68
Art of the Dance (The), xiii, 11–12, 88, 91
art critics, 86
artistic revolution, 5, 97, 108
arts academies, 6, 28
arts, xii, xiii, 7, 8, 9, 18, 19, 21, 23, 24, 33, 40, 45, 46-50, 67, 72, 74, 80, 91, 92, 98, 108
audience, 39, 40, 41, 43, 44, 45, 63, 69, 81

B

back-to-nature movement, xii, 4, 43, 78. *See* nature.
ballet, xii, 9, 11, 17, 19, 21, 26, 28, 29, 36, 39, 46, 47, 51, 57, 59, 62, 64, 68, 69, 72, 88, 89, 108
Ballroom dance. *See* popular dance.
barefoot dancing, xiii, 11, 15, 35, 36, 46
Beaumont, Cyril, 9, 84, 86, 87, 92, 93
Beegle, Mary, xi, xii, xiii, 9, 13-14, 16, 17, 26, 31–32, 33, 40–42, 44, 50, 59–60, 62, 69, 74, 75, 78, 80, 84, 96, 99–100, 101, 102, 103, 108, Plates 1-6, 28
Bergson, Henri, 31, 33
body, xiv, 18, 20, 27–36, 37, 47, 50, 55, 57, 60, 61, 63
Book of the Dance (The), xiii, 103–106, Plates 40-48
books, xi, xii, xiv, 9–10, 18, 19, 20, 80, 82-86, 92, 94, 98
brain, 27, 28, 74, 77; rational, 32, 37, 44. *See* mind-body dichotomy.

C

Caffin, Caroline, 90
Caffin, Charles and Caroline, xi, xiii, 86, 90-94, 95, 96, 103, 108. Plates 24, 27-32
Camera Works, 90, 95-96, Plates 25-26

M

Magriel, Paul, 9, 84, 85
Manual of Dancing (A), xiii, 17, 70, 79, Plates 84-85
Manual of Gymnastic Dancing, 53, Plates 51-52
Marey, Elienne Jules, 31, 52
Margaret Morris Dancing, xiii, 19, 85, Plates 19-23
Martin, John, 11, 22, 94
media. *See* books and photographs.
mind-body dichotomy, 28, 31, 32, 34, 35, 37, 61, 64
Modern Dancing and Dancers, xiii, 86–89 Plates 33-39
modern dance theory, xii, xiii, 77-81
Moller, Helen, xii, xiii, 4, 5, 14-16, 20, 24–25, 32, 42-44, 45, 49, 51, 60, 75, 78, 85, 86, 95, 100, 102, 108, 109, Plates 12-17
Morris, Margaret, xii, xiii, 12, 16, 17, 18-20, 26, 35–36, 45–46. 49, 50, 51, 63–65, 71, 74, 75, 80, 85, 86, 95, 101, 102, 103, 108, 109, Plates 18-23
movement, xiii, 13, 18, 30, 34, 52, 61; fundamentals, 18, 33, 61, 65, 71
muscles, 26, 31, 35, 64, 68, 73
muscular Christianity, 3
music, 9, 15, 19, 22, 24, 26, 40, 42, 43, 45, 46, 47, 48, 49, 53, 55, 61, 71, 79, 81, 84, 85, 88, 108
Muths, Gut, 53-54

N

natural dancing, xiii, 4, 14, 19, 23, 24, 56, 59, 80; natural movements: walking, running, 60; hopping, skipping, xiii, 29, 35-36, 42, 54, 58, 59, 60, 61–62, 63, 64, 65, 73, 107
naturalism, 30
nature, 28-29, 42, 54, 67, 77, 79, 101, 108
notation, 19, 71, 72-73, 84

P

pageantry, pageants, 13, 23, 42, 45, 46, 56, 60, 100
Parker, Francis, 7
Pavlova, Anna, 89, 105, Plate 41
pedagogy. *See* education.
Pennington, Jo, 106, Plates 80–81, 83, 87–89

R

S